Eight Simulations
Controller's Book

# Eight Simulations

For upper-intermediate and more advanced students

Controller's Book

*Leo Jones*

Cambridge University Press
Cambridge
London   New York   New Rochelle
Melbourne   Sydney

Published by the Press Syndicate of the University of Cambridge
The Pitt Building, Trumpington Street, Cambridge CB2 1RP
32 East 57th Street, New York, NY 10022, USA
296 Beaconsfield Parade, Middle Park, Melbourne 3206, Australia

First published 1983

Printed in Great Britain
at the University Press, Cambridge

ISBN 0 521 28839 8  Controller's Book
ISBN 0 521 28838 X  Participant's Book
ISBN 0 521 24591 5  Cassette

MU

# Contents

# Acknowledgements

Thanks to everyone who helped to try out and later revise the original versions of these simulations. In particular, thanks to: Richard Denman, John Forster, Perrée Geller, Sue Gosling, Belinda Harris, Jan Milburn, Michael Roberts and Rob Shave for all their advice, comments and criticisms. Without the inspiration of the *Nine Graded Simulations*, written by Ken Jones and originally published by the Inner London Education Authority (re-published by Max Hueber Verlag 1982/3), the simulations for foreign students in this book could not have been conceived.

The author and publishers are grateful to the following newspapers, press agencies, publishers, picture libraries and individuals who have given permission for the use of copyright material: *The Daily Telegraph, The Guardian, The Observer,* Reuters, Associated Press, The Press Association Ltd, British Broadcasting Corporation, Barnaby's Picture Library, Michael Holford, Popperfoto, Spectrum Colour Library, Heinemann Educational Books Ltd, Longman, Macmillan Education Ltd and Oxford University Press.

It has not been possible to identify the sources of all the material used and in such cases the publishers would welcome information from copyright owners.

Cover photographs by Nigel Luckhurst

# Introduction

## What is a simulation?

A simulation is a representation of a series of real-life events. The classroom represents the setting where the events take place. The events are accelerated and simplified to fit them into the time available and to ensure the maximum amount of language activity.

*roles*    The participants are expected to work without their teacher's supervision and their success or failure will be a result of their own efforts. In most of the simulations the participants will be given roles to play but this does not mean that they have to be brilliant character actors to succeed. The roles they play may involve them in adopting a new surname (but not first name) and a new profession and sometimes new opinions, but it will not involve them in pretending to be someone with a different personality. In other words, no dramatic talents are required – simply an ability to adapt to an unfamiliar situation.

*involvement*    A simulation isn't just a 'game' where everyone has a good time and tries to be the winner. The involvement every participant feels in the tasks they have to do means that for a few hours a simulation can seem just like real life, where everyone is responsible for their own decisions and actions and shares in any collective decisions taken, too.

Like real life, a simulation is usually open-ended – there are no 'right answers'. What happens in the end depends on the decisions and actions of the participants.

## What is the purpose of a simulation?

The main purpose of a simulation is to provide an opportunity for the participants to practise a full range of language skills. Most normal classroom practice and discussion concentrates on a fairly narrow range of language skills – in fact such practice is often guided by the teacher to concentrate on specific lexical items or specific structures. In a simulation participants find themselves using all the English they know to achieve their aims – just one step away from what will happen to them in real life.

In a simulation the participants will be using their English

1

creatively and purposefully. They will be concentrating on their communicative tasks, not on formal accuracy. This kind of fluency practice is just as important as practice which helps students to speak accurately.

*skills*      In a simulation, the participants will find themselves doing different activities, using different language skills and performing different communicative functions. For example, they may begin by reading a newspaper article, then listen to a radio broadcast, then meet in groups to discuss the article and the broadcast in the light of other information they have received, then make a plan or reach a decision, then try to persuade the members of another group to agree to their plan or decision, and finally put forward the plan or decision to a public meeting. This complex integration of language skills is one of the most valuable aspects of a simulation. Again, this is a realistic requirement, since in real life each language skill isn't isolated in the way it often is in simple classroom activities.

*feedback*      A simulation can also provide extremely valuable feedback on students' progress. They can be monitored while they are in the process of actually communicating and not, as often happens in classroom language practice, trying hard not to make mistakes – or playing safe and avoiding areas of potential difficulty.

*meaningful*      Above all, the discussion and language activity which goes on in a simulation has a *purpose*. And because it has a purpose it becomes meaningful. Communication takes place because it needs to take place. The simulation becomes a kind of temporary reality – the nearest you can get to reality in a classroom, perhaps.

*participants*      Since a simulation develops its own momentum and stimulates the participants' imaginations and concentration, it can continue uninterrupted for several hours, after which it is quite normal to hear participants say: 'We forgot we were talking English – but we were, weren't we?'

## Who are these simulations for?

These simulations are designed with foreign learners of English in mind. They involve students in more talking and listening and less reading and writing than simulations designed for native speakers. However, a balance is still maintained between these four skills, and the more time-consuming reading and writing is done at home before and after the simulation itself, to allow more talking during valuable class time.

They are equally effective with any number of participants between ten and thirty. They have all been tested with mixed-ability groups of intermediate (pre-FCE) and advanced (post-

CPE) students as well as with classes of equal-ability students. They work particularly well with combined classes of similar levels. This has two main advantages: first, the groups can be made up both of classmates who know each other well and also relative 'strangers' from another class (which adds to the realism of the activity); and second, more than one room is very useful for a simulation.

## How do the simulations in this book work?

Each simulation can be divided into three distinct phases: *preparation, the simulation* itself and *follow-up*. This is explained in the diagram below and then in more detail in the two sections that follow.

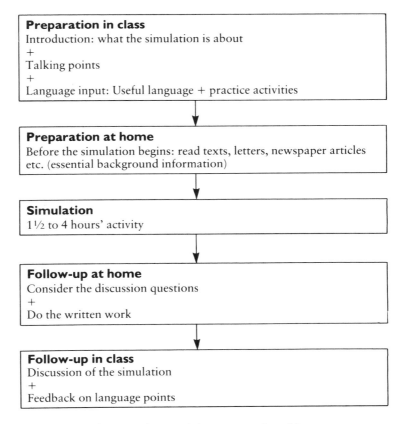

**Preparation in class**
Introduction: what the simulation is about
+
Talking points
+
Language input: Useful language + practice activities

**Preparation at home**
Before the simulation begins: read texts, letters, newspaper articles etc. (essential background information)

**Simulation**
1½ to 4 hours' activity

**Follow-up at home**
Consider the discussion questions
+
Do the written work

**Follow-up in class**
Discussion of the simulation
+
Feedback on language points

In the simulations, the participants are placed in groups or teams, given *role information sheets* or other information, and then they discuss how they are going to deal with the situation they have been placed in. From that point, different information is given or different combinations of participants are made which influence the decisions that have already been made. These eight simulations are all different and it might be misleading to generalize further about them, but a quick look at the descriptions of each simulation will give a satisfactory overview.

*preparation*    You'll need one or perhaps two lessons before each simulation starts for the preparation – the notes in this Controller's Book tell you what needs doing. An advanced class may not need so long.

*the simulation*    For the simulation itself, you'll need at least 1½ hours and no more than 4 hours. If you can arrange three or four lessons in a block, that would be ideal. (To do this you may have to rearrange your normal timetable or swop lessons with a colleague.) The 1½-4 hour period should *not* be interrupted by breaks, which might disturb concentration or destroy the atmosphere which has been built up. The variety of activity and the intensity of involvement obviate the need for breaks, even in a 4-hour stretch.

*follow-up*    After the simulation has finished you will also need a lesson for the follow-up discussion. This is an essential part of the simulation, since it allows the participants to discuss their success as communicators, to tell each other what they personally did and to relate the simulation to their real-life experience. The follow-up discussion can take place another day, after the written work has been done.

*difficulty*    The eight simulations are not graded in terms of language difficulty, but the earlier ones are less complex than the later ones. In this sense, there is a progression from easy to difficult but this does not mean that they should necessarily be done in sequence. If you or your participants haven't done much role-play before, then it is a good idea to start off with *Anglebury* before you tackle *World News Magazine*. You'll find both of these fairly easy to organize and the Controller's notes for them are the most detailed of all. However, your students will not find either of them 'too easy' to do. In other words the sequence of the simulations is an indication of how much the Controller has to do, rather than of how much English the participants are expected to know. The later simulations, such as *The Arts Centre*, may seem more risky because of their complexity – particularly if you don't know your participants very well. Nonetheless, you'll find that the unpredictability of the later simulations makes them very exciting for all concerned.

*photocopying*    For each simulation you'll need to photocopy some pages from the Controller's Book to give out to the participants when the simulation begins. The idea of using photocopies, rather than printing all these 'documents' in the Participant's Book is to keep the essential surprise element. Not knowing exactly what is going to happen is part of the design of the simulations. In some of them, in fact, the participants should be kept in the dark about the theme of the simulation before it begins. The other reason for using photocopies is to create an 'information gap' between the different participants: if participants are given different information, they then have the chance to communicate this to each other; but if they all already know each other's information, through its being printed in the Participant's Book, there is no point in communicating it.

## How is the Participant's Book organized?

The format of the Participant's Book is similar in each simulation:

### What the simulation is about

There is a brief description of the simulation and some advance information in the form of a picture.

### Talking points

The questions start the participants talking about some of the themes of the simulation to whet their appetites and to help you to decide who might be best suited to certain roles.

### Useful language

In each simulation one or two areas of language are revised which will help the participants to communicate more effectively. This isn't of course the *only* language they'll need.

### Practice activities

The useful language is practised in some activities which are different from those in the simulation.

### Before the simulation begins

There are several pages of texts: letters, newspaper articles and documents or maps. The participants must read these carefully beforehand so that they possess the necessary background information to do the simulation.

### Follow-up discussion

There are questions for the participants to consider which will focus their attention on what they were doing and what they have learned from it.

### Written work

There are 3 written assignments based on each simulation. It is important to insist on one of these being done to exploit the involvement that was generated in the simulation itself.

Take a look at the *Anglebury* simulation in the Participant's Book to see how the format works in the most straightforward simulation.

## How is the Controller's Book organized?

The format of the Controller's Book is also similar in each simulation:

### Description

An overview of each simulation is given, including some information which the participants must not be given until later.

### Assigning roles and arranging groups

There are detailed instructions on how the participants should be arranged in groups. It is a good idea to take special care when doing this to ensure that each group is 'well-balanced', with a mixture of abilities, ages, men and women, personalities and nationalities in each group. Some groups may need a good organizer as their team-leader.

### Organizing time and arranging space

There is advice on how to fit each simulation into your timetable together with specimen timetables as a guide. There is also advice on how the room or rooms you are using should be arranged.

### What you need

There is a list of the (simple) equipment you need and of the photocopying that has to be done in advance. Also any other preparation required is noted here.

### Preparation

There are step-by-step instructions on how to deal with the talking points, useful language and practice activities.

### The simulation

There are detailed step-by-step instructions on how to organize and control the simulation from start to finish. There is also a complete transcript of what is on the cassette.

### Follow-up

There are step-by-step instructions on how to deal with the follow-up discussion.

### Pages for photocopying

The role information sheets and some other documents are printed only in the Controller's Book. These have to be photocopied and given to individual participants according to the step-by-step instructions.

A quick look at the *Anglebury* simulation in the Controller's Book will show how this format works in the most straightforward simulation.

## What is on the cassette?

In the simulations the cassette is used either to start everything off or as a source of information while the simulation is going on. The following items are on the cassette:

*Anglebury*
two Radio Budmouth news broadcasts

*World News Magazine*
yesterday's programme (as a guide for the participants)

*The Bridge*
Radio Meryton news broadcast

*People in the News*
five telephoned reports

*The Arts Centre*
five 'rumours'

*Green Isle*
Radio Northbridge news and Radio Lymport news.

## What does the Controller have to do?

The most important part of the Controller's job is *not* to
interfere but to let the participants deal with their own problems
and difficulties. Once a simulation is under way the participants
*behaviour*   must be allowed to be responsible for their own behaviour. The
only time when you must actually step in is if things are really
getting out of hand. However, if you have formed well-balanced
groups there is very little chance of there being any discipline
problems: a participant who talks to a friend in his mother
tongue will be stopped by the other members of his group and a
team-member who doesn't pull his weight will be reprimanded
by the rest of the team. Very rarely, however, there may be the
odd case of the participant who refuses to participate sensibly.
He should be taken aside (on a pretext appropriate to the
simulation: 'message from Head Office' or 'the Mayor wants to
see you') and asked what the problem is. Possible solutions
might be to assign him a different role in another group, or to
make him Assistant Controller, or he could even be released to
work on his own elsewhere. As long as the other participants are
still actively involved in the simulation, there's certainly no point
in stopping the whole thing, just because one or two participants
are dissatisfied.

*supervising*   Apart from not interfering, there is another more active part
of your job: to issue the photocopied role information sheets
and other documents, to play the cassette at the appropriate
times, to keep track of what's going on by popping into the
rooms from time to time and eavesdropping on the participants
and to make notes of not only the errors you overhear, but also
of the language which impresses you. You will also have to keep
an eye on the clock and make sure the participants keep to any
deadlines they have been given.

*anxiety*   The first 20 to 30 minutes of a simulation are always worrying
for the Controller. You wonder if the simulation will get off the
ground, if it will last long enough, if the participants will be
capable of doing the task they have been set and so on. In spite of
this, it is probably the worst time to step in and offer advice. The
participants need time to solve their own problems by themselves.
Part of their job is to decide on courses of action — and making
decisions often involves moments of silence for contemplation
and planning. Changes of pace are important in a simulation
and 4 hours of frenetic activity is not what you're aiming at.

*preparation*    Another thing you have to do is to arrange the preparation for the simulation. Make sure your participants know roughly what they're going to do (without giving away any of the surprises) and that their English is adequate for the needs of the simulation. You will need to decide how much revision of the useful language and how many of the Practice activities are going to be helpful for your class, and whether any further language preparation is needed (particularly for vocabulary). With a very advanced class, the Useful language can sometimes just be read through and the Practice activities omitted. In some cases you may find the Practice activities can be used as follow-up instead of as preparation. When the simulation is over, you will also have to lead the follow-up discussion. There is more detail on these points in the step-by-step instructions for the *Anglebury* simulation.

*setting up*    Before the simulation begins, there will be a fair amount of arranging to do: a schedule, equipment, rooms and photocopying. You will have to decide on the role each participant will be playing, or the team he or she is in. It's best not to tell the participants which roles they'll be playing until the simulation is about to start. There are two reasons for this: one is that there will be an element of surprise and the other is that if anyone is absent on the day of the simulation, the roles can be rearranged on the spur of the moment without inconveniencing the participants. Another thing you will have to do is read both the Participant's Book and the Controller's Book so that you are familiar both with what the participants are going to read before the simulation and what they are going to be doing during the simulation.

## Conclusion

*using English*    Using the simulations will be a challenge for your students: they will be doing more than just practising their English because they will have decisions to make and problems to solve. They will be *using* their English to achieve their aims in the simulation – thinking in English, discussing in English and working in English – and this is the closest they're likely to get to real-life working in English inside a classroom.

*roles*    The participants don't need to be good actors. They are often given roles to play in these simulations, but they are still 'themselves within the role'. They should behave as they would behave in the given situation. The Role information sheet gives each participant an outline of the role he or she is to play. However, all the details of the role will come from the participant's own experience, ideas and personality, as well as from his or her interpretation of the background information and reaction to the events that occur during the course of the simulation. (To help them to realize this, you should make sure that in the roles they are given, they keep their *own* first name. For example a student called Maria Mantovani, playing the role of someone called 'Arnold' becomes 'Maria Arnold' in the simulation, and this is what is written on her role information sheet and on her badge, if she has one.)

*low profile*    The simulations may also be something of a challenge for you. Although you are the Controller, you stop being 'The Teacher' during a simulation. It's the participants in a simulation who are the active ones. The Controller should basically keep a low profile, keep in touch with the action, but try not to influence or dominate the events in any way. It is essential that the participants realize that they are 'on their own', which means that they are responsible for their own work. The Controller is not a 'parent-like' teacher during a simulation, but simply the organizer of the simulation. It may sometimes be necessary to offer extra help or advice to some participants who are in difficulty, but try to make sure that they don't rely on you to help them out of every subsequent difficulty.

*instructions*    If you haven't done a simulation before, it's a good idea to start with *Anglebury*. The Controller's notes for this are particularly detailed and they explain and justify the techniques being used. The later simulations may seem very complicated at first glance, but this is part of their appeal and it is what makes them exciting to do. They have all been tried out and the step-by-step instructions make it clear what to do at each stage. You will be surprised to find that, once a simulation is under way, it develops its own energy and reality. It starts to 'run itself' and this will free you to monitor your students' performance. Once the participants have got involved in what they are doing, they become determined to succeed in their tasks and 'make the simulation work well'.

I hope you enjoy these simulations as much as my students have done and that your students find them equally useful and stimulating. It's not until you actually *do* a simulation that you realize quite how powerful a technique it can be.

# Anglebury

## Description

This is the most straightforward of the simulations in this book. It is a sort of 'easy introduction' to doing a simulation for the first time. So, if your class has a lot of experience of this kind of work and has done a lot of role-play, *World News Magazine* or *The Bridge* might be better to begin with.

In this simulation there are five groups of participants, each representing different groups of Anglebury townspeople. After they have studied the background information given in the Participant's Book, the participants hear a news broadcast and then receive their role information. The groups then meet in separate areas for discussions. There are five plans to consider which may solve Anglebury's traffic problem, but the first decision the groups have to make is their attitude to the Anglebury Parents' Association's 'Day of Action' in protest against the County Council's indifference to the situation. A second news broadcast announces that this has been called off and that there will be a public meeting the same evening. Each group then decides which plan they will recommend and what strategy they will adopt at the public meeting. At the meeting the groups make their recommendations and a vote is taken to decide on the most acceptable plan.

## Assigning roles and arranging groups

All the simulations in this book can be used with any number of participants from ten to thirty. It can be very rewarding to combine two or more classes together for a simulation: the participants can benefit from having to communicate with 'strangers' and the simulation can be more of a 'special event' than a normal language lesson. An extra classroom is handy, too.

In Anglebury there are five groups of townspeople, each consisting of a minimum of two and a maximum of six participants. So, with a total of ten students each group would have two members, with twelve students two groups would have three members each and three groups would have two members each, and so on. The roles and groups are shown below:

| Group A PARENTS | Group B POLICE AND COUNCILLORS | Group C SHOPKEEPERS | Group D RESIDENTS | Group E FARMERS AND INDUSTRIALISTS |
|---|---|---|---|---|
| Anderson | Burke | Carter | Davis | Evans |
| Allen | Bailey | Chapman | Donaldson | Emery |
| Alexander | Barker | Clarke | Duncan | Ellis |
| Adams | Barnes | Curtis | Dixon | Edwards |
| Andrews | Barrett | Crawford | Dean | Eaton |
| Arnold | Bell | Cole | Daniels | Eastwood |

The participants should use their own first name with the surname of the role they have been given.

In deciding which participant is to play which role, try to match the experience, opinions and personality of your students to the roles. The Talking points discussion (Participant's Book page 4), before the simulation begins, will help you to find out more about your students' opinions.

To make the first part of the simulation go well, try to have two strong personalities in the Parents group. Apart from this, simply make sure each group has a good balance: different personalities and abilities in each.

The role information is on pages 20 to 27. This should be photocopied and cut up. The roles at the beginning of each group are more important than the ones nearer the end. So with a smaller number of participants than thirty, you can discard the less important roles. This doesn't mean that in a group of, say, six shopkeepers that Crawford and Cole are necessarily roles to be given to the weakest students in the group. Each role is important in its way.

## Organizing time and arranging space

*Preparation*    The reading of the guidebook extract, the discussion of the Talking points and the language preparation in the useful language and practice activities should be done at least one day before the simulation. This work will take about 45 minutes to cover. The students should be told to read the background information at home before they do the simulation.

*The simulation*    The five groups need separate areas to meet in, so furniture may have to be rearranged. If you have more than one room available, some of the groups can meet in separate areas of different rooms:

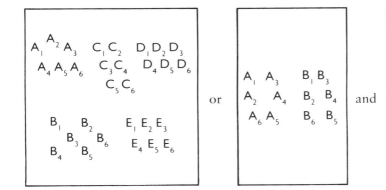 or 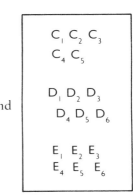 and

For the public meeting all the participants reassemble. If possible, arrange the seats in rows facing the front like a public hall. The councillors can sit facing the audience.

This simulation is less complex than the later ones, so it can be completed in 1½ to 2 hours. 4 hours for this simulation would be too long. How long you and your participants spend will depend on exactly how much time you have available. As a guide, here is a specimen timetable for this simulation:

9.00   Play the first news broadcast and
       give out role information.
9.10   Group meetings begin.
9.10   Play second news broadcast.
       Group meetings continue.
10.00  Public meeting begins.
10.30  Voting at the meeting.
       Short break (or stop here for today).
10.40  Begin follow-up discussion.
11.00  Stop.

At a pinch, this simulation could be done in an hour, but with a large number of participants it should be stretched to two hours plus follow-up the next day.

*Follow-up*  The actual discussion might take 20 to 30 minutes, but remedial language work would add to this.

## What you need

Photocopies of the role information (pages 20 to 27) with your
   participants' first names added.
A cassette player.
The *Eight Simulations* cassette.

## Preparation

*What the*
*simulation*
*is about*

1 Using page 4 of the Participant's Book, introduce the simulation. Don't give any extra information which might spoil any surprises in the simulation (like the Parents' 'Day of Action' plans).

2 Ask the students to read the guidebook extract, making sure they understand it. There's no need to ask detailed comprehension questions or to 'exploit' the text. Just make sure they've taken in the information.

*Talking*
*points*

3 Look at the talking points together. Put the class into groups to discuss the questions for a few minutes. Then reassemble as a class and ask each group to give their views. The aim of this discussion is just to start them thinking and talking about some of the themes of the simulation, so don't spend too long going into detail because the simulation will be doing this. Encourage the students to talk about their own country.

*Useful*
*language*

4 A very advanced class may not need to do the useful language and practice activities sections, though a quick run-through might be useful revision. Most classes do find this kind of language preparation helpful and it provides a repertoire of expressions which they can use in the simulation. Of course, these expressions are only a very small part of the equipment they need to communicate effectively.

   Get the class to look at the expressions. Make sure they can pronounce them easily and that the meaning of each is clear. Ask for suggestions on how each incomplete sentence could continue. For example,

*It'd be a good idea to...    ... do some practice before we do*
*the simulation.*

*Practice*
*activities*

5 Divide the class into groups of 3-4 students. Ask them to decide together how they would solve each of the problems on page 5 of the Participant's Book. Go round monitoring each group and offer advice and correction when necessary.

6 When most of the groups are ready and have finished solving the problems, form new groups so that each new group contains one member from each of the earlier groups:

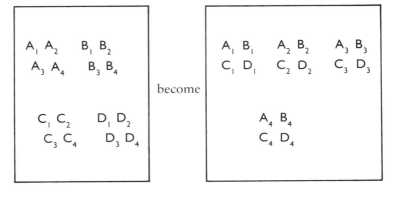

If necessary, there can be two members of an earlier group in a new group. Each student has to 'announce' his or her group's decisions to the new partners. Again monitor each group correcting and advising. When most of the groups are ready, discuss the activity with the whole class reassembled.

*Before the simulation begins*

7   Make sure everyone reads the information given on pages 6 and 7 of the Participant's Book before they do the simulation. Point out that if anyone forgets to do this, they'll be holding everyone else up in the simulation itself. This reading should be done for homework. A quick skim of the text in class beforehand might be useful and might give the students a chance to ask any questions they have on the text.

## The simulation

1   Play the first Radio Budmouth local news broadcast on the cassette to the assembled participants. This will set the scene and provide some more important background information. Here is a transcript of the broadcast:

*Newsreader:*   ...four cars were involved but no one was injured. In Anglebury there has been more controversy over the traffic situation in the town. The Anglebury Parents' Association is planning a 'Day of Action' this Saturday. All traffic through Anglebury will be stopped by a protest march of parents and children and by a sit-down in the town centre. The sit-down may stop all traffic for 24 hours from midnight on Friday. Our reporter, Mark Johnson, is in Anglebury and here is his report:

*Johnson:*   This is Mark Johnson in Anglebury. I'm speaking to one of the leaders of the Parents' Association. Mrs Atkins, as secretary of the association, what are your association's plans for this weekend exactly?

15

| | |
|---|---|
| *Mrs Atkins:* | Well, Mark, the traffic situation has been deteriorating here in Anglebury over the past few years. The County Council have refused to take any action and the time has come for the people of Anglebury to show the authorities that they mean business and that they will not tolerate the situation any longer. |
| *Johnson:* | But surely this proposed sit-down is going to cause far more inconvenience to your fellow-townspeople than to the authorities? |
| *Mrs Atkins:* | There will be inconvenience, yes. But we have no other course of action open to us. We propose to sit down in one of the main roads through the town and to stop all traffic for 24 hours. Believe me, it's no joke living in Anglebury. Last month Rachel Appleby was killed on her way to school by bicycle and 5 children were injured when a lorry ran out of control down the High Street on Monday. |
| *Johnson:* | Thank you, Mrs Atkins. ...I'm now at Anglebury police station where I have with me Inspector Blenkinsop. Tell me, Inspector, what is your view of the parents' proposed 'Day of Action'? |
| *Blenkinsop:* | Well, Mr Johnson, we regard the proposal as highly irresponsible. Next weekend is Bank Holiday weekend and traffic is likely to be particularly heavy. Many holiday-makers will be on their way to Knollsea and even if they could be diverted round the back streets of the town, there would be mile-long queues. The police have a duty to ensure that the highway is not obstructed, though of course we have no objection to a short march or demonstration being held. |
| *Johnson:* | Do you agree that the traffic situation in the town is dangerous? |
| *Blenkinsop:* | There have been a lot of accidents, yes, but there are better ways of protesting than sitting down in a main road. |
| *Johnson:* | Inspector Blenkinsop, thank you. Various plans have been suggested to solve the problem. One of them is the reopening of the Anglebury to Knollsea railway. I shall be talking to the Chairman of the Knollsea Railway Preservation Trust in our afternoon pro-gramme tomorrow. This is Mark Johnson returning you to the studio. |
| *Newsreader:* | Thank you Mark. And finally the weather: this afternoon, sunshine can be expected... |

2  Give each participant his or her role information, photocopied from pages 20 to 27. Allow time for them to read this and if requested play the news broadcast again. Make sure everyone has read the plans in the Participant's Book and that they have the plans in front of them. Finally, make sure everyone knows exactly what they have to do.

3  Put the 5 groups into their separate areas (or rooms). Make

sure that each group knows what they're supposed to be doing – the role information explains this. Leave the groups to begin their meetings.

4 The group meetings take place (lasting 15 to 20 minutes). If you wish to monitor each group, do this very discreetly: don't interrupt or interfere at all. Make notes of the language points you can mention in the follow-up discussion. It's probably better at this stage *not* to monitor and to stay out of the way so that each group can begin unsupervised.

5 After 15 to 20 minutes of the group meetings, stop everyone and inform them that Radio Budmouth is just about to broadcast another news programme.

Play the second Radio Budmouth local news broadcast on the cassette. Here is a transcript of the broadcast:

*Newsreader:* Radio Budmouth news on the hour. There has been a new development in the Anglebury traffic controversy. Over to Mark Johnson in Anglebury for a report.

*Johnson:* Thank you. The County Council have just made an announcement that there will be a public meeting in Anglebury Town Hall this evening to discuss the plans for solving the traffic problem in the town. All interested parties are urged to attend the meeting and to make their views known. The Council promise speedy action provided that agreement is reached at the meeting on which of the plans to adopt. The Parents' Association have called off their 'Day of Action' for the time being, but Mrs Atkins said to me a few minutes ago that it will still take place if the Council don't take the immediate action they have promised. This is Mark Johnson returning you to the studio.

*Newsreader:* And now the rest of the news. The elephant house at...

6 The five groups continue their meetings but now tell them to concentrate on deciding which of the plans on page 7 of the Participant's Book their group will support. Make sure each group has the plans in front of them. They should also decide on the strategy their group will adopt at the meeting later. Again you might want to monitor each group, but do this unobtrusively – make notes of mistakes and don't interrupt to correct them at the time. Don't participate in any of the discussions yourself.

The meetings continue for 25 to 40 minutes. Make sure you tell the participants in advance exactly when the public meeting is to take place. This time is their deadline for the group meetings.

7 After 25 to 40 minutes, stop the groups and arrange the seating for the public meeting. The Councillors can sit facing the members of the public. (With a small number of partici-

pants they can be joined by the police on the 'platform'.) In this simulation it is probably best for you, the Controller, to take the chair at the meeting. You can be the 'Minister of Transport' or the 'Mayor of Anglebury'. By taking the chair yourself, you can make sure that everyone has a chance to speak if they want to, that each group has time to put its recommendations forward and that no one dominates the meeting. (Alternatively, one of the Councillors can chair the meeting – but make sure he or she is well briefed beforehand.)

The meeting lasts 25 to 45 minutes. Before closing the meeting, take a vote on which plan is to be adopted. Some discussion may be necessary to decide how the voting is to be arranged. This may be quite complicated if it has been agreed to combine any of the plans.

8  If your follow-up discussion is to be on a later day, set the written work now and ask the participants to think about the discussion questions before you meet next. The advantage of having this discussion later is that the delay enables the participants to take a more dispassionate view of the simulation. The written work will also help to focus their minds on what they did.

However, since this first simulation is relatively simple compared to the more complex ones later, no great harm will be done by having the follow-up discussion immediately after the simulation. But at least take a 10-minute break before you start!

## Follow-up

1  See 8 above.

*Follow-up*  2  Make sure everyone has read the questions. If there hasn't
*discussion*  been much time for consideration of them since the simulation, start the discussion in groups to get things going. After about 10 minutes call the groups together for a general discussion.

3  There are three objectives in the follow-up discussion:

   a)  To let the participants analyse their performance as communicators and talk about the difficulties they had.
   b)  To give *you* time to point out to them where their weaknesses lie, to correct the mistakes you heard and to suggest remedial work.
   c)  To let the participants discuss the wider issues arising from the simulation and compare the simulation with real-life situations they have experience of.

Without leading the discussion too dictatorially, try to make
sure that all three objectives are achieved.

*Written work* 4 Set the written work (do this immediately after the simulation
if your follow-up is the next day). Allow the participants to
choose which task to do or decide together with the class
which one everyone is to do. Make sure everyone understands
exactly what is required of them as regards content, style and
length.

    The written work is easy to forget after a very eventful
simulation, but there are several important reasons why it
should be done:

a) It gives the participants a chance to put into writing some
of the ideas they were only able to express in speech in the
simulation.

b) The content of simulation written work is often more
meaningful than compositions set on other work, simply
because the participants become very involved in what
they are doing. This mental and emotional involvement is
worth exploiting to stimulate written work in which the
students really have some ideas they want to communicate.

c) The simulation concentrated on speaking, listening and
reading. Writing was neglected.

**ANDERSON** – member of Anglebury Parents' Association

*You have four children (James and Clive, age 14, Richard age 10 and Roger age 8). They have to cross the main A347 to get to school.*

Decide where to sit down on Saturday to block the traffic.

**ALLEN** – member of Anglebury Parents' Association

*You have two children (Lucy age 18 and Jonathan age 14). They both cycle to school and this is getting more and more dangerous.*

Decide where to sit down on Saturday to block the traffic.

**ALEXANDER** – member of Anglebury Parents' Association

*You have one child (Sally age 10). One of her classmates was injured by a lorry on the A347 on her way home from school.*

Decide where to sit down on Saturday to block the traffic.

**ADAMS** – member of Anglebury Parents' Association

*You have three children (Billy age 7, Tom age 4 and Anne age 2). You drive Billy to school on your way to work – the traffic is awful!*

Decide where to sit down on Saturday to block the traffic.

---

**ANDREWS** – member of Anglebury Parents'
Association

*You have three children (Peter age 10, Paul age 8 and Jane age 6).
You live just round the corner from the school and the road in
Plan D would pass extremely close to your home.*

Decide where to sit down on Saturday to block the traffic.

---

**ARNOLD** – member of Anglebury Parents'
Association

*You have two children (John age 15 and Mary age 11). They both
walk to school and have to cross the main A206 at the traffic lights
in the High Street.*

Decide where to sit down on Saturday to block the traffic.

---

**BURKE** – Head of County Police Traffic Division

*The traffic hold-ups at weekends are getting worse and worse.
With your small force you can do nothing to enforce the 30 mph
speed limit in Anglebury.*

Decide on your attitude to the proposed 'Day of Action'.

---

**BAILEY** – County Councillor

*The traffic problem is not as serious as the parents claim. Any
solution would be very expensive. It's only in the summer that
there are delays to traffic through the town.*

Decide on your attitude to the proposed 'Day of Action'.

---

**BARKER** – Police Sergeant

*You have witnessed many accidents in Anglebury involving pedestrians, cyclists and children. There are too many heavy lorries driving down narrow streets too fast.*

Decide on your attitude to the proposed 'Day of Action'.

---

**BARNES** – County Councillor

*The situation is very bad in Anglebury, but the Council cannot afford to do anything in the next few years.*

Decide on your attitude to the proposed 'Day of Action'.

---

**BARRETT** – Police Constable

*The traffic hold-ups in the town make drivers very impatient and more likely to take risks and cause accidents.*

Decide on your attitude to the proposed 'Day of Action'.

---

**BELL** – County Councillor

*The only course of action is to spend money to solve the town's problem and as quickly as possible.*

Decide on your attitude to the proposed 'Day of Action'.

---

**CARTER** – owner of supermarket

*Your local customers park outside your shop in the High Street. 25% of your trade is from holidaymakers driving through Anglebury in the summer.*

Decide on your attitude to the proposed 'Day of Action'.

---

**CHAPMAN** – owner of gift shop

*80% of your trade is from visitors to the town who notice your shop as they are driving through.*

Decide on your attitude to the proposed 'Day of Action'.

---

**CLARKE** – owner of antique shop

*70% of your trade is from visitors to the town. You have your own car park and most of your customers come to Anglebury especially to visit your shop.*

Decide on your attitude to the proposed 'Day of Action'.

---

**CURTIS** – owner of newsagent's shop

*One of your paperboys was knocked off his bicycle by a lorry last week. A lot of your trade depends on both local people and visitors being able to park outside your shop in the High Street.*

Decide on your attitude to the proposed 'Day of Action'.

---

**CRAWFORD** – owner of sweetshop

*You are losing customers because of all the heavy traffic thundering past your shop all the time.*

Decide on your attitude to the proposed 'Day of Action'.

---

**COLE** – owner of café

*50% of your customers are motorists who park outside your café in the High Street.*

Decide on your attitude to the proposed 'Day of Action'.

---

**DAVIS** – local resident

*You have lived in Anglebury all your life. It used to be a pleasant town. Now the traffic has made it intolerable.*

Decide on your attitude to the proposed 'Day of Action'.

---

**DONALDSON** – local resident

*You used to live in London. You have bought a house away from the main roads in Anglebury. Plan C would bring the bypass past your back garden.*

Decide on your attitude to the proposed 'Day of Action'.

---

**DUNCAN** – local resident

*You have lived in Anglebury for ten years. Your house is on the main A347 near the town centre. The traffic is bad and it is often difficult for you to cross the road.*

Decide on your attitude to the proposed 'Day of Action'.

**DIXON** – local resident

*You have lived in Anglebury for several years. The heavy traffic doesn't bother you but you work in Budmouth and the hold-ups sometimes make you late for work.*

Decide on your attitude to the proposed 'Day of Action'.

**DEAN** – local resident

*You have lived in Anglebury all your life. You remember the old railway to Knollsea – there weren't any traffic problems when it was still open.*

Decide on your attitude to the proposed 'Day of Action'.

**DANIELS** – local resident

*You live just north of the station. Plan C would demolish your house.*

Decide on your attitude to the proposed 'Day of Action'.

---

**EVANS** – farmer

*Your farm is just beside the River Frome. The road in Plan D would cut your farm in half.*

Decide on your attitude to the proposed 'Day of Action'.

---

**EMERY** – industrialist

*Your factory depends on rapid road transport. At the moment the heavy traffic makes all deliveries to and from your factory unpredictable.*

Decide on your attitude to the proposed 'Day of Action'.

---

**ELLIS** – farmer

*Your farm is just north of the River Trent. The road in Plan C would cut across part of your farm but you would get good compensation for this. You could do with the extra capital at the moment.*

Decide on your attitude to the proposed 'Day of Action'.

---

**EDWARDS** – industrialist

*Your factory is outside the town on the Budmouth road. Most of your trade goes through the port of Budmouth and a bypass would not affect your trade.*

Decide on your attitude to the proposed 'Day of Action'.

---

**EATON** – farmer

*Your farm is divided by the A314 north of the River Trent. The heavy traffic makes it difficult to get your cows and farm machinery across the road. Last year two of your cows were killed.*

Decide on your attitude to the proposed 'Day of Action'.

**EASTWOOD** – industrialist

*Your factory workers are always late for work in the summer because of the traffic. They travel in by bus and car from the surrounding villages.*

Decide on your attitude to the proposed 'Day of Action'.

# World News Magazine

## Description

The participants are divided into teams, each preparing a 'news magazine programme' based on an input of newspaper cuttings. These cuttings are on pages 36 to 51; they should be photocopied, cut up and handed to each team one by one at intervals throughout the duration of the simulation. The programmes are recorded for playback to the whole class afterwards. The recording of the programmes is done 'live' with no pauses or interrruptions. The programmes can be radio broadcasts using a tape recorder or, if video is available, TV broadcasts.

The simulation gives the participants valuable experience of reading English newspaper articles purposefully and of working under pressure in an English-speaking team.

## Assigning roles and arranging groups

There are no roles to be given in this simulation, but during the course of the simulation the participants will be role-playing newsreaders, reporters and assorted interviewees. It might be a good idea to nominate a producer for each team to act as team leader – someone who can be relied on to keep the team working together in a not-too-bossy manner. Or, each team can elect their own producer.

With thirty participants, three teams with ten in each will work well; with only ten participants, keep the element of competition by having two teams of five participants; with twenty participants, three teams of six or seven are probably best – and so on. Make sure each team is well-balanced with a mixture of personalities, different nationalities, men and women, and students of different ability in each of the teams. It is a good idea to combine two or three fairly similar classes together, if this is possible, to make the simulation more of an 'occasion' and to give the students a chance to work in a team with 'strangers' as well as their familiar class-mates.

## Organizing time and arranging space

*Preparation*  For the talking points, useful language and practice activities
you'll need 45 to 90 minutes, depending on how thoroughly you
want to do the practice activities. If you're combining classes for
the simulation, they don't need to be combined for the preparation.

*The simulation*  Ideally, you need an uninterrupted period of 3 to 4 hours for the
simulation, including recording time. With only 1 ½ to 2 hours
at your disposal, there are too many news items, so you will
need to discard some of them. If your participants expect to be
given breaks, persuade them that this is not a good idea since
it'll make them lose concentration and waste time. If necessary,
refreshments could be brought to the teams or collected by a
member of each team on a tray.

The programmes themselves should each be 10 minutes long.
You need to allow 5 minutes before each recording for everyone
to get ready. With two teams, the programmes can be 15
minutes long if you have enough time. Don't be too rigid about
timekeeping during the recordings – allow a programme to run
over by a minute or two if necessary.

Each team needs its own area to work in. A large classroom
can be divided quite easily into two or three areas by moving the
furniture around. If possible, though, each team should have a
separate room. The rooms needn't all be classrooms – one could
be an office or a common room perhaps. If you can also get a
large table for each team to sit round, it will help the working atmosphere.

The deadlines for each team will need to be staggered if all the
programmes are to be recorded on the same equipment in a
central 'studio'. In the specimen timetable below, 3 teams are
working towards staggered deadlines and doing the simulation
in 3¾ hours. This will need to be adapted to your own circumstances, of course.

9.00  Play yesterday's *World News Magazine* on the cassette.
9.05  Each team goes to its room or area.
      Issue first three or four news items.
      Continue issuing news items one by one at intervals of a
      few minutes right up to about 15 minutes before each
      team's deadline.
12.00  First team's deadline.
12.05  Record first team's programme.
12.15  Second team's deadline.
12.20  Record second team's programme.
12.30  Third team's deadline.
12.35  Record third team's programme.

(The first and second teams are allowed to leave after their recordings are finished. Only the team which is actually making its recording is allowed in the studio.)

If each team is given its own tape recorder and microphone to make the recording on, the whole process is simplified and the three teams can each work to the same deadline. The programmes must still be recorded live and not built up on the tape bit by bit.

If you only have 1½ hours for the simulation, it is simplest to have the teams working to the same deadline by providing each with a tape-recorder and issuing only about half the news items. In this case your timetable might look like this:

19.00  Play yesterday's *World News Magazine*.
19.05  Each team goes to its own room or area. Issue first three or four news items and continue issuing news items until about 20.00.
20.15  Deadline: each team starts its recording of a 10-minute programme.
20.30  Set written work. End of simulation.

*Follow-up*   The playback session will last about as long as the programmes took to record (20 to 35 minutes). However, if you intend to pause the tape frequently when playing back the recordings, more time should be allowed. The follow-up discussion will add 15 to 25 minutes to this time.

## What you need

Two or three photocopies each of pages 36 to 51 (newspaper cuttings), cut up, ready to give out during the simulation. A 4-hour simulation might need all the newspaper articles, but a shorter one needs fewer. This means that you can check through all the articles beforehand and discard any that appear to be too difficult for your participants or which are unlikely to interest them.

A cassette recorder and the *Eight Simulations* cassette.

Audio or video recording equipment. *Or* each team can have its own cassette recorder with a blank cassette. If possible, a cassette recorder for each team to use for rehearsal is useful in any case.

A dictionary (English-to-English) for each team.

Your own schedule of deadlines for each team and a list of the members of each team.

Two or three copies of an English newspaper (preferably recent) if you want to add some up-to-date cuttings to the ones in the book.

## **Preparation**

*Talking*    1   Look at pages 9 and 10 in the Participant's Book and spend a
*points*           few minutes on the talking points. Get the discussion started
               in groups before having a short general discussion. Don't
               spend too long on this.

*Useful*    2   Look at the expressions together. Make sure everyone can say
*language*        them easily. How would they finish the incomplete sentences?

*Practice*    3   Divide the class into 2, 4 or 6 groups of 3 to 5 students. Get
*activities*       half of the groups to look at the newspaper article on page 11
               of their books and the other half at the one on page 12. Each
               group should read their article and summarize it in note form.
               Go round giving help if requested. A class with little experience
               of doing this may need a great deal of help.

         4   Each group should rewrite their notes into a brief report. One
               member of the group can be secretary. Again go from group
               to group offering advice. Encourage co-operation between
               groups by getting them to read each other's reports and
               comment on them. (If your class have not written many
               summaries like this before, it may be necessary to offer some
               guidelines before they start.)

         5   Each group prepares and then role-plays interviews with
               people mentioned in their article. Some groups may need
               your advice here. For example, people in the first article who
               could be interviewed are:
                  George Fursman or another coach passenger
                  Mr and Mrs Masters
                  A Shepton Mallet police officer
               And in the second article:
                  Brian Milton, the competition organizer
                  One of the pilots, perhaps the winner
                  Kenneth Messenger, a hang-glider manufacturer

         6   Get each group to perform one or more of their interviews in
               front of the rest of the class. Ask for comments: would the
               interview be the right length for a broadcast and would it be
               interesting enough?

*Before the*    7   Make sure everyone reads the information on page 13 of their
*simulation*      books before they come to the simulation. Emphasize that
*begins*          this preparation is essential, otherwise time will be wasted on
               the day of the simulation.

## The simulation

1 To show the participants how their programme might
sound, play yesterday's *World News Magazine* on the
cassette. (A group of very advanced or very confident
participants may not need this.) Here is a transcript of the
broadcast:

(music)

*Presenter:* Hallo and welcome to World News Magazine! In
today's programme we have an interview with
Clint Eastwood, a report from our correspondent
in China and an interview with a survivor of the
volcanic eruption in Venezuela – not forgetting
the news and weather, of course. But first a
report from David Green in France.

*David Green:* This is David Green at Le Touquet Airport in
Northern France, where passengers are just
coming off the Aer Lingus Boeing 737, which
was hijacked on a flight from Dublin to Heathrow.
The hijacker has just been taken away by the
police for questioning and I have with me one of
the passengers, Mrs Jane Thompson. Mrs
Thompson, can you tell us just what happened?

*Mrs Thompson:* Yes, well, it was a perfectly normal flight to begin
with until this man – one of the passengers – got
up from his seat near the back of the plane and
went with one of the stewardesses to the flight
deck. As far as we could tell, he didn't have a gun
or anything. Anyway, the next thing we heard
was an announcement from the captain saying
we were not going to land at Heathrow. He was
about to say where we were going instead, when
another voice interrupted him and then there was
a lot of shouting and then the intercom went dead.

*David Green:* What happened then?

*Mrs Thompson:* One of the stewardesses came out and told us to
fasten our seatbelts and then a few minutes later,
we landed here.

*David Green:* What was the reaction of the passengers?

*Mrs Thompson:* Well, there was no panic at all among the
passengers, even though no one really knew what
was going on. Everyone just sat and talked and
some people were reading and this went on for, I
suppose it must have been about 2 hours until the
man came out with the captain and .. um .. well,
there were two women with babies and an old
lady and they were allowed to leave the plane.

*David Green:* Can you describe the man?

*Mrs Thompson:* Yes, he had these wild, sort of mad-looking eyes
and he had long hair and his clothes were all wet
and smelt of petrol. And he kept shouting and
waving his arms about.

| | |
|---|---|
| *David Green:* | About 6 hours later a force of anti-terrorist police stormed the plane and arrested the hijacker. How did you feel when the doors burst open? |
| *Mrs Thompson:* | I'm afraid by that time I was fast asleep. The person sitting next to me was shaking me and telling me to wake up. She told me we were safe and free. So I got up and walked down the steps and here I am. |
| *David Green:* | Mrs Thompson, thank you. This is David Green returning you to the studio. |
| *Presenter:* | Thank you, David. And now over to Janet Miles, here in the studio. |
| *Janet Miles:* | Hallo. We welcome to the studio Clint Eastwood, who is here in London for the British premiere of his new film. Mr Eastwood, you are the star of the film and you produced and directed it yourself. That's quite an achievement. Can you tell us something about the film? |

2  Assign the participants to their teams. Each team should have its own separate room or area to work in. Either nominate a Producer for each team or get each team to elect a Producer as its first task. The Producer's job is to make sure everyone participates equally in the preparation and the broadcast.

3  Tell the teams how long their programme is to be (10 or 15 minutes). Inform them when their deadlines are for the broadcast later. Make the deadlines 5 minutes earlier than the actual time the recording starts, so that any last minute panic can be absorbed and not hold up the next team's recording. If each team is to record its programme in the same central 'studio', the deadlines need to be staggered.

4  Give each team an English-to-English dictionary, if possible.

5  Give each team their first batch of news items (about 4 to start with). Cut them up before giving them out. Before leaving the teams to start work, make sure everyone knows what they have to do. A quick re-reading of the information in their books on page 13 is advisable.

6  Continue delivering the remaining news items one by one to each team while they are working. Ignore cries of 'We've got enough now!' Tell them that you can't stop the world but remind them that one of the most important parts of their task is the selection of news items for the broadcast. Point out that some of the later items may be much more interesting than some of the earlier ones and that there's no time to use them all. This means they may have to abandon work they have done earlier and therefore it is very important that they select the items they wish to use.

7  If you have some copies of 'today's' newspapers, pick out a

few topical articles from them. Cut them out and add them to the ones you've photocopied from this book. There will be time to make this selection once the teams have started work.

8   Time should be spent monitoring each team at work. Try to be as unobtrusive as possible and resist the temptation to participate yourself. If you can, sit apart from the team and make notes for a few minutes before moving off to issue another news item and monitor another team. If you have combined classes and there is another teacher available, one of you can be Controller while the other monitors each team. While you are monitoring, you will also be able to gauge how each team is getting on with their work. This may lead you to stop issuing news items to an overburdened team, for example, or to issue several items immediately to an underemployed team. Such decisions will depend on how your participants are coping – there is no point in issuing every single news item, if doing so will cause a team to give up in despair!

9   About 20 minutes before each team's deadline, issue the last news item. Make sure each team has time for a final rehearsal before they go on the air. (The last of the news items are unlikely to be used in the programme, so it's a good idea to rearrange the newspaper cuttings so that the ones which will interest your class most are issued early, and the less interesting ones are issued last.)

10   If the teams are doing their broadcasts simultaneously in separate 'studios' (using their own tape recorders in separate rooms), make sure the equipment is working properly by doing a brief test run with each team before they start their broadcast.

   If the teams' deadlines are staggered and each team is going to record in the same 'studio', do a brief test run before the first team arrives. Check the microphone and the recording level.

11   With staggered deadlines, take the first team to the studio to record their programme. The other teams should not be present while they are recording. If you're using video, make sure the camera operator knows who is going to be the next one to speak during the programme (the next speaker can nod or wave to the camera operator before he comes on camera, for example.)

   Record the second and third programmes without allowing the first team to be present. Give them a break, let them go early (but tell them about **12** and **13** first!) or ask them to tidy up the room they were working in.

12   When all the programmes have been recorded, let the

participants know when the recordings will be played back.
13 Set the written work. Ask the participants to think about the
follow-up discussion questions before you next meet.

An interval between recording the programmes and playing
them back and discussing the simulation is advisable. It will help
the participants to take a more dispassionate view of what they
did. The written work will also help them to do this. However
the playback session could be done after a lunch break, for
example. After a short coffee break the participants might still
be too emotionally involved to be ready to discuss the simulation.

## Follow-up

*Follow-up* 1 Begin with the follow-up discussion. Make sure that the
*discussion*  participants talk about the whole of the simulation, not just
the 10-minute broadcast. Make your own comments on
language points you noticed and suggest remedial work if
necessary.
2 Play back the recordings. It's probably best to play each one
without interruption and save comments for later, rather than
keep on pausing the tape.
 *Don't* comment on broadcasting technique or programme
quality. The participants are not professional broadcasters!
But do comment if they succeeded in communicating effectively. Give praise as well as criticism.
3 Set the written work, if you haven't already.

# Siberian oil claim amazes West

By John Andrews,
Energy Correspondent

The Soviet Union — the world's largest oil producer — has discovered an oil field in Western Siberia many times bigger than the rest of the world's proven oil reserves put together, according to Petro-Studies, a Swedish oil consultancy firm specialising in Soviet oil matters.

The size of the claim provoked incredulity in western oil circles and a statement from the Central Intelligence Agency in Washington that "our people still stand by their basic assessment" that the Communist block countries will be net oil importers by 1983.

The PetroStudies claim, which immediately depressed oil shares on the London market, is that a new field near the existing Samotlar field con tains 619 billion tonnes, equal to 4.55 trillion (million million) barrels of 35 gallons each.

The PetroStudies director, Mr Mitja Jermol, said yesterday that the report was based on Soviet oil publications and that the oil was high-quality light crude and not very deep in the geological structure.

PetroStudies, which is to publish a full version of the report on Monday, says: "The Soviets have called this a unique natural phenomenon. There has been nothing to approximate such a find before."

That is something of an un- derstatement. If the claim is correct the field is seven times bigger than the 650 billion barrels of proven reserves calculated by BP for the world.

On the 50 per cent recovery rate calculated by PetroStudies, the field would double the amount of ultimately recoverable world reserves estimated by this year's World Energy Conference.

Major oil companies yesterday harboured no nightmares of cheap Soviet oil flooding the world to make North Sea investment and research into coal and nuclear conversion worthless. One executive laughed: "We think it's just crazy." A spokesman for Standard Oil of California said: "Initially, I guess, we react with incredulity."

The incredulity would be justified even if PetroStudies has misplaced a decimal point. The largest field found so far is the Ghawar in Saudi Arabia's eastern province. With estimated reserves of 70.5 billion barrels, Ghawar stretches 150 miles in length and 25 miles in width — making the mind boggle at the extent of the alleged Siberian field.

PetroStudies says that the Soviet Union is already changing its exploration and development policy because of the new find. But the CIA doubts the production potential and the Soviet Union's ability to master the required technology. For the moment, at least, OPEC still rules.

# Down in Hampshire a star is born

By Martin Walker

A self-taught astronomer without O levels or formal educational qualifications, yesterday became one of the three living people in Britain to have a star named after him.

Mr David Branchett, a 26-year-old production worker at the Pirelli cable factory at Eastleigh, Southampton, spotted the exploding star which is henceforth known as Nova Branchett 1981 through a pair of binoculars from his bedroom window.

He said yesterday: " I thought I had let everybody down at first. I reported it to the British Astronomical Association, and they organised a special watch by enthusiasts around the country at dawn the next day, but it was too cloudy.

" The day after that, the sky was clear. But nobody could see it, not even me—and we had much better equipment than the binoculars I had used at first. But that evening I heard from the Royal Observatory at Greenwich that they, had recorded an image of my star on a photographic plate."

The International Astronomical Unit in the US was then alerted. Two American observatories scanned the sky and performed a spectrum analysis, and confirmed the nova.

"It was just part of my routine patrol", Mr Branchett said. "I get up before dawn every morning, and I know the sky fairly well, so when I saw the new star I knew right away that this was unusual. It had gone nova — a star that had exploded. I was just lucky at catching it at its peak intensity".

Mr Branchett, who has always prided himself on his eyesight, is thought to have made astronomical history. His was the faintest visual sighting ever made.

" I am quite lucky here, about 186 feet above sea level, a good all-round horizon and about five miles north of the town so there is little pollution. But I only saw it for about three minutes before the dawn started to gather," he explained.

The star is about 1,000 light years from earth, in our own galaxy, a part of the Milky Way. Specific distances, and the intensity of the nova itself, will have to await further spectrum analysis from the US.

"The binoculars I use are very powerful, but still the kind of thing you can see at race meetings. Anything bigger would be too heavy to hold for long periods," said Mr Branchett, who has been an astrology enthusiast for 13 years.

"It must be one of the few ways in which an amateur with ordinary equipment can still beat the professionals with their giant telescopes. How else would I get anything named after me ? Now I have a whole star."

# Japan to help build new Suez Canal

From Robert Whymant
in Tokyo

Japan is to play a leading role in building a second Suez Canal, parallel to the existing one, according to a study submitted to the Egyptian Government.

Conforming with Washington's pressure to support US global policies in the Middle East and in areas bordering conflict, Japan has recently been increasing aid to Egypt, Pakistan, Turkey, and Thailand.

Tokyo's commitment to the new Suez project, on which a final decision is expected later this year, is outlined in a report by the Japanese Ministry of Transport, commissioned by the Egyptian Government. Official sources say that Japan will supply manpower, technology, and financing amounting to an eventual $1.25 billion over 14 years.

This will be the second Suez expansion programme dominated by the Japanese. The first widening and dredging project was completed last year, with Japanese capital amounting to 43 per cent of money from foreign sources.

Widening the waterway from 297ft to 480ft and deepening it from 43.5ft to 58.5 ft, has recently made possible the passage of 150,000 ton vessels (fully loaded) and 370,000 tons (unloaded) compared with 70,000 and 250,000 tons respectively before.

Japanese participation accounted for 70 per cent of the entire operation and it is thought that Japan will play a similar role in the new project. The Japanese recommendation is for the opening of a 100-mile canal running alongside the existing one, so that the waterway can handle two-way traffic. The Sutz Canal is only a single lane at present.

Japan believes that its economic and technological assistance to Egypt will contribute to stability in the Middle East and will not worsen its relations with Saudi Arabia, its main oil supplier. The Japanese Government only agretd to take part in President Carter's request, two years ago, for West German and Japanese loans to reward Mr Sadat for the conclusion of the peace treaty with Israel.

## HEAT TOLL NEAR 600
**By Our New York Staff**

As the death roll in America's Southern states neared 600, officials said many of the victims were old people afraid to leave doors or windows open because of fear of intruders.

# Package flight to the surgeon

By Hugh Hebert

Alongside all those colourful invitations to exotic places like Bath and Bond Street, British Airways offices round the world are about to offer brochures for the most expensive and painful package tours in the business.

A traveller from Tokyo can have 22 days in London, with full board, for the knock-down price of £10,550, including a couple of new heart valves. ClinicAir, says the brochure, brings you to Britain "for the finest medical care at guaranteed prices." In some cases this "may be combined with a holiday or business trip."

The packages have been put together by BA and American Medical International, which runs a string of private hospitals in Britain, including the Harley Street Clinic and the Princess Grace hospitals in central London. It is planning to have half a dozen more.

Dr Stanley Balfour-Lynn, chairman of AMI (Europe) told a press conference to launch the scheme that the 60 or 70 doctors involved were all "top consultants from London teaching hospitals."

They had agreed to reduce their normal private practice fees so that the costs of the packages could be held down, he said. But the doctors, not surprisingly, have insisted that this should not be revealed to patients by giving a breakdown of the package costs, because their British-based patients will be paying the full rate.

The package price for a heart operation is only £9,350 if the patient is coming from Malta, or £9,750 from Kuwait.

A hysterectomy patient arriving from Athens — 18 days in London — will pay £4,150, and for stripping varicose veins (one leg, eight days) the cost for a traveller from Singapore is £3,200. Prices for treatment at hospitals in Windsor or Harrow are lower.

The numbers of Middle Eastern patients arriving for treatment in Britain's burgeoning private hospitals have dropped sharply, so the medical companies are keen to find new sources of business.

One of the main targets for the BA/AMI is the expatriate Britisher who, like most people who fall ill abroad, feels that he would like to return home for treatment.

# Melbourne mix-up

A Melbourne man returned home, started to undress, and found that his wife was in bed with another man. Indignant at the interruption, the other man chased the husband down the street. Both were wearing only slacks and socks.

The husband crashed into the owner of a jewellery shop who was standing outside his store pointing a gun at a burglar he had surprised leaving through a broken window. The shop owner thought the husband was an accomplice of the burglar, and fired at him, narrowly missing him.

The other man leaped to the defence of the husband, and attacked the jeweller. The police arrived, broke up the melee, and arrested the three battlers.

The burglar escaped, unscathed but empty-handed.

# Jumbo pilot aborts Heathrow landing

By Philip Jordan

A British Airways jumbo jet from Hongkong with 399 passengers aboard was forced to abort a landing at Heathrow yesterday only feet off the ground after the captain saw a Pan Am jumbo on the runway.

The incident has been reported to the British Airports Authority, but it does not qualify as a "near miss."

It happened at 10 a.m. as flight BA 020 was coming in to land with Captain Gordon Buxton at the controls.

One passenger said: "We could only have been about 10 yards off the ground when the engines went to what seemed like full power and we climbed straight back into the air again."

The plane circled Heathrow for 15 minutes before landing. Another passenger said: "Even as we were banking away we saw an Air France plane land on the runway below us. The time between flights must be very small."

Captain Buxton apologised to his passengers for what he described as the "leap into the air" because of "an obstruction on the runway."

As the plane circled, he told the passengers the obstruction had been a Pan Am jumbo which had been slow taking off.

A British Airways spokesman said last night that Captain Buxton had made the manoeuvre on his own initiative. A report on the incident would be prepared by Captain Buxton and a copy would go to the British Airports Authority.

The spokesman said that the usual gap between planes landing and taking off at Heathrow at busy periods was about two minutes. Separate runways were usually used for take-offs and landings but yesterday, possibly because of pressure of traffic, one runway was being used for both.

## WOMAN TRIED TO GIVE DRIVING EXAMINER £60

A woman who tried to give her driving examiner a £60 present as she sat in the car before her test, was fined £50 yesterday. Mrs Sakue Tsubouchi, 43, handed the examiner a packet containing three £20 notes and told him it was a Christmas present.

When he tried to return it she told him she had to pass the test because she needed to take her children to school, Mr Clifford Groves, prosecuting, said at Bromley.

Mrs Tsubouchi, of Caroline Close, Croydon, pleaded guilty to offering corruptly the money to Mr Michael Beecroft to pass her in the test at West Wickham last November. She was also ordered to pay £65 costs.

## Short hair, please

MORE than 600 men were refused entry into
Singapore last year because their hair was too
long. Another 800 were allowed in after agreeing
to have their hair cut, according to Home Affairs
Minister Hua Sian chin.                    *Reuter*

IAN BRADSHAW

India comes to Somerset : South Pether-
ton is now used to the sight of businessman Victor Lamont peddling his friends
around town in a rickshaw.

His firm, Global Village Crafts, is
currently importing some of the three-
wheeled machines which are advertised
as 'The taxi of the future . . . guaranteed
to last into an age when petrol is no
more.'

The rickshaws sell for £325, and a
London store is using two of them for
local deliveries. Other buyers include a
Devonshire man strong enough to haul
his family along country lanes at weekends.

# Spike in the wheels

From AP in
Irvine, California

A lorry driver dropped a load of wide-headed, inch-long roofing nails on a San Diego road and at least 100 motorists had flat tyres as a result, official here said yesterday.

Only 29 drivers involved in the incident last Friday had reported tyre damage to the California highway patrol by yesterday morning but Officer Gary Keller said he expected calls from at least 100 people. "Somebody's going to have to pay for this and it isn't going to be cheap," the policeman said.

He said traffic backed up in the southbound lanes for six miles for more than two hours as at least 100 vehicles had flat tyres.

# Cousins get 10p damages

From AP in Paris

The French appellate court has ordered the Canard Enchaine to pay one franc (10p) each to two cousins of President Giscard in a libel case stemming from an article the newspaper published on a diamond scandal. A year ago, it published an alleged photostat of a letter signed by the deposed Emperor Bokassa ordering the gift of a 30-carat set of diamonds to Mr Giscard. The two cousins, Francois and Jacques Giscard were connected to the scandal in an article the investigative weekly published. The headline suggested that the affair was a "French Watergate."

# O-level for girl, 9

By a Correspondent

A NINE-year-old girl who has never been to school has become the youngest person in Britain to pass an O-level examination. Ruth Lawrence obtained a Grade A in the O-level maths paper, and finished the exam half-an-hour early.

A spokesman for the joint matriculation board in Manchester said yesterday: "we have checked our records, and as far as we can tell she is the new British record-holder for an O-level pass of any kind. The previous youngest was a 12-year-old boy from Glastonbury who passed an O-level when he was 10."

Ruth has been taught by her parents at their home in Halifax Old Road, Huddersfield, and her father, Mr Harry Lawrence, a computer consultant, said: "She has been ready for the exam for a year or two.

Ruth is now preparing for her A-level in maths with her father, who used to teach the subject. "We will probably wait a while before she takes it. She wants to give herself the best chance of getting a distinction."

# Walk-out by Customs men

MORE than 300 Customs men based at Heathrow Airport will leave their posts for five hours today to attend a mass meeting of civil servants in London.

The 1 p.m. walk out by members of the Society of Civil and Public Servants will leave only a handful of managerial staff in the airport's three passenger terminals and cargo area. The meeting is in protest over the Government's Civil Service pay policy.

## Give it a Ms

VERY few women in the US—16 per cent—use the " Ms " designation, according to a recent poll. The overwhelming majority prefer the traditional designations, " Miss " or " Mrs," according to the 1980 Virginia Slims American women's opinion poll. The survey also found that attempts to " desexualise " job titles have not been very successful. Asked whether a woman should be called a " milkman," a " milkperson " or a " milkwoman," 35 per cent said " milkman," 31 per cent " milkperson " and 27 per cent " milkwoman."—AP.

# Staying in the warm at the nick

By Nick Davies

It should have been a great escape: nice and dark, not a guard in sight and all the cell doors left open. But when the time came on Monday night, most of the prisoners in Great Yarmouth police station apparently decided it was just too cold to bother.

Only four of the eleven men there took advantage of the slack security at the station where they are being held on remand because of the prison officers' dispute. Last night the four men were still at large.

Their seven fellow-inmates were in their warm cells with the doors still swinging ajar. Police say the cells are too small to cope with the extra prisoners during the dispute and the doors have to be left open to provide ventilation.

"We have to cater for two needs," said Chief Superintendant Peter Howse. "We have to keep people in secure conditions, but we also have to consider the humanitarian aspects. There is normally only one man in each cell."

Since the dispute began 14 weeks ago, some of the eight cells in the police station have housed four men at a time. "We had many complaints of headaches and people feeling ill," said Mr Howse. "We decided we had to leave the doors open during the night, but that means the first line of security is non-existent."

The only other line of security is a door which leads from the cell block to the exercise yard. It is thought that prisoners had filed down the bolts on this door so that they would not lock properly.

Soon after 3.45 a.m. yesterday station officers completed one of their routine inspections — and Ernest Baldwin, aged 24, Kim Cox, 22, Alexander Dow., 36, and Sheldon Petrie, 24, slipped through the door into the centre of Great Yarmouth.

It was only four degrees above freezing The rain and sleet which had been falling all night had stopped but a stiff wind was still blowing in from the sea. Their seven mates declined the offer of freedom.

The hardy four, who were awaiting trial on burglary charges, are thought to have walked for about ten miles before catching a bus into the outskirts of Norwich. A bus driver has contacted police with details.

More than 100 prisoners have escaped from police cells since the prison officers' dispute began early in October. About a quarter of them are still at large.

## £80,000 raid at Harrods

THREE armed men got away with more than £80,000 from Harrods store in Knightsbridge, London, yesterday. Two Security Express men were collecting the store's takings in the basement security office when the three men broke in wearing Harrod's security officers' coats.

## 'Dinosaur lives'

A FAMILY of dinosaurs may still be alive in the Congo, two US scientists said in Dallas, Texas, yesterday. Mr Roy Mackel of Chicago University, and Mr James Powell, a Texas-based zoologist and explorer, said that the theory was based on witness accounts given to them on an expedition to the Congo and on reports of earlier explorers. — Reuter.

## Ancient spectacles found during dig

THE EARLIEST pair of spectacles ever found in Europe have been discovered by archaeologists digging in the City of London. They will be displayed at an exhibition to be mounted by the Council of British Archaeology in London on Friday.

The spectacles, which date from the 15th century, were designed to be clipped on the nose. The lenses are missing. The frames are made of bull horn.

# Couple's bad dream holiday

DAVID PEARL and his girlfriend, Amanda Luper, arrived home from America yesterday after muggers had put an end to their holiday, and fell into the hands of another thief.

Disaster first struck when Miss Luper, aged 18, of Mill Hill, north London, went for a walk on Sunset Boulevard in Los Angeles. She was mugged by three men who stole over $1,000, a £350 gold necklace, and a ring.

So the couple returned to Heathrow, and more trouble. A man aboard their plane offered to help Miss Luper with her luggage. But he ran off as they were disembarking, taking her purse containing £111

Mr Pearl, of Southgate, north London, had paid for the trip with redundancy money

# Civil servants 'work only two hours a day'

From George Armstrong
in Rome

CIVIL SERVANTS in five Italian ministries work only two hours a day — or 12 hours a week — rather than the 36 hours for which they are paid, according to a report commissioned by Mr Massimo Severo Giannini, who has been given the task of improving the workings of the central administration.

Mr Giannini's survey of the five ministries also showed that only 34.5 per cent of the staff said they were " never " without something to do in their offices, while 56.5 per cent said that " now and again " they were idle, and 9 per cent said that " often " they had nothing to do.

When asked what they did when they had nothing to occupy themselves in the Ministry, 56 per cent of those at the Ministry of Posts said that they made telephone calls. That may go towards explaining that Ministry's general and particular indifference to the handling of letters.

At the Ministry of Education, 64.7 per cent said that they read " journals " which, in Italian, includes not only newspapers but the more widely sold Mickey Mouse and Donald Duck magazines and the all-time ministerial favourite, weekly magazine of crossword puzzles.

At the Ministry of Agriculture, 66.7 per cent of the staff said that when idle they turned to " conversation " within the ministerial walls, while at the Ministry of Transport, 14.3 per cent said that they took up knitting and crocheting. Another 28.6 per cent at Agriculture said that they did things outside the office, and 20.5 per cent at Education did another job but within the Ministry.

None of these idle hours, or the hours spent outside their ministries, are included in the separate report on absenteeism. The civil servant with nothing to do is not absent. He is, however, absent on the average of 12 per cent of the days he is expected to work.

He also is allowed, by contract, to be legally absent from his desk for two months of the year " for serious motives," which can mean pregnancy, maternity, paternity, or, the most common complaint, " nervous exhaustion."

Many Italian civil servants hold a second job. They may even be employed by their own Ministry do do a second job, or they may work in the afternoons for a private firm.

# Split-second advantage of the left-hander

From Paul Webster
in Paris

IF TENNIS court surfaces get any faster, left-handed John McEnroe may eventually dominate right-handed Bjorn Borg for the simple reason that left-handed sportsmen in general have naturally quicker reflexes.

French sports researchers are convinced, after 15 years of experiments, that the growing domination of left-handers in tennis, particularly on synthetic courts, can no longer be put down to their unorthodox technique.

According to a team led by Dr Guy Azemar at the National Physical Education Institute, everything points to left-handers having several thousandths of a second more time to react.

The researchers, including a nerve specialist and a specialist in sciences related to sport, were struck by the disproportionate success of left-handers, particularly in tennis and fencing. Left-handers dominate at the top although 90 per cent of people are right-handed. Of the world's 200 top tennis players, 16 per cent are left-handed, but five of the top 20 and three of the top four are left-handers.

Borg, therefore, is considered to be an exception — a right-hander who can make up with technique what he loses in reflex. Before the French research, it was presumed that he fought against the odds arising from unorthodox technique. He is forced to change his game to receive backhands, while left-handed opponents have a marginal advantage in a points system that favours unorthodox serv-ing at game point.

Dr Azemar found that left-handers were even more dominant in fencing, particularly with the foil where speed and precision at close quarters is crucial. Three out of four fencing gold medals at the Olympic Games were won by left-handers who took all of the first eight places in the men's foil. This advantage dictates the composition of the French foil team, which Dr Azemar has been looking after for the past 15 years.

His research team is convinced that the advantage is explained by the way messages are carried from the brain. "We want to show that the sort of information needed in sport — speed and direction of attack — are treated by the right-hand side of the brain which handles the organisation of time and space," he said. "With left-handers the message is transmitted direct to the left-hand side of the body. With right-handers the message travels through the left-hand side of the brain first, the side which treats logic. Then it passes to the other side causing a loss of thousandths of seconds."

Dr Azemar said that a series of exercises were being developed to prove the theory and to make a strict division between what left-handers gain by their unorthodoxy and what they gain by quicker reflexes. He thought that the exercises might prove that right-handers reverse the balance on slow courts, where Borg is still king, because the yhave more time to work out "elaborate strokes" devised by the brain's logical side.

# The drink smuggler will score

## by ROGER KERR

THE INGENUITY of the Scottish football fan in getting drink into matches is likely to defeat new legislation planned to stop drunkenness and violence on the terraces.

Gloomy police yesterday claimed that the Scottish fans' ability to smuggle in drink 'makes Papillon look like a learner.'

From next month fans will be committing an offence if they try to enter a ground while drunk, or in possession of alcohol or cans and bottles likely to cause injury. It will also be an offence to be drunk on a coach going to or from a match or to carry alcohol on a coach.

The tough new legislation, announced last week by Mr Malcolm Rifkind, H o m e Affairs Minister at the Scottish Office, will mean maximum penalties of 60 days in prison and/or a £200 fine. The legislation covers 53 football grounds in Scotland as well as Murrayfield, the international rugby ground in Edinburgh.

Although Mr Rifkind and the Scottish football establishment claimed that the legislation will mean no extra policing, the police think otherwise.

Sergeant Joe Black, general secretary of the Scottish Police Federation, said:

'It is our belief that all football grounds shoud be licensed like any other place of public entertainment, and that the clubs should be responsible for the behaviour of spectators.'

Sergeant Black felt that increased police activity would only alienate the police from the public. ' The fans are well-practised in smuggling drink into the grounds. They secrete alcohol in places around the body that make you wonder. It will be very interesting to see just how much alcohol is consumed after 2 February.

# Scots island rabbit cull

Residents of a remote Scottish island have banded together to fight thousands of rabbits ravaging farmland.

An estimated 100,000 rabbits are attacking farmland on the tiny Orkney island of Rousay, stripping grass at the rate of 40 tons a day.

Farmers are now to get help from public funds to set up a £27,000 three-year programme to reduce the number of rabbits.

Their cash will be matched by grants from the Highlands and Islands Development Board and Orkney Islands Council, will pay for a full-time rabbit control operator.

Gassing, snaring, and netting will back up the farmers' shooting programme. The main target will be a heather-clad central hill on the 15,000-acre island from which rabbits make forays to cultivated land.

Mr Christopher Soames, secretary of the rabbit clearance society, said : " It is a terrible problem. Ten rabbits can eat as much as one sheep. and there are estimated to be 100,000 rabbits here."

47

# Storms hold up Everest ascent

STORMS have delayed the eight-man British climbing team attempting the first ever Everest ascent in winter and without oxygen.

The expedition is now hoping that the Nepalese Government will extend their licence to be on the mountain.

Yesterday THE OBSERVER received this despatch sent on 11 January by Paul Nunn from Camp Two, 23,000 ft. up Everest.

"We had established Camp One on the Lho La ice plateau and fixed ropes 3,000 ft. up the west shoulder of Everest.

"Alan Burgess and I reached the site of Camp Two on 2 January and dug a tent platform late in the afternoon.

"We erected a MacInnes box tent in the last hour of light. This is a nylon tent stretched over a very strong tubular alloy frame.

"At 23,000 ft. it is so cold that a shovel and an ice axe shattered when we were chopping out a shelf in the snow.

"The westerly wind is incessant, but we have had some magnificent winter views.

"We made tea and settled down in conditions too crammed and cold to be restful. Outside only inches separate the box tent from the vast ice slope that falls away to Lho La.

"The wind strengthens overnight and we sleep little. The morning is clear and gusty, but a night of deep frozen insomnia makes it difficult to start fixing

**PAUL NUNN of the British Everest winter assault team reports from Camp Two at 23,000 ft.**

rope up the easier angled slope to the west shoulder, especially as we risk being blown away.

"The weather is so wild that gusts are not expected. Yet after two o'clock Joe Tasker arrived and we dug a second platform for a dome tent, sited above the box. It was a struggle erecting it. The high wind threatened to snatch away the fabric and two poles shattered in the extreme cold. Only the arrival of Brian Hall enabled us to balance the tent on its undersized ice shelf.

"As darkness fell Pete Thexton arrived with a load. He seemed unconcerned at the prospect of a long descent by torchlight, involving 27 abseils to the Lho La plateau.

"That night we slept badly again. Early the next day we tried to improve the position of the dome tent and to protect it with igloo-style snow blocks, conscious that one tent had already been destroyed by wind.

"That night there was a very bad storm and the dome tent was destroyed by the wind.

"We are neither cheered nor downcast to hear from the Italian expedition on Everest that our project is thought to be impossible."

# Polar man falls into crevasse

### by ROBERT LOW

THE THREE-MAN Transglode expedition team trying to cross Antarctica are now less than 400 miles from the South Pole.

Last week they survived their worst accident yet when radio operator Charlie Burton, above, plunged into a crevasse on his snowmobile. It was the type of accident they had been fearing ever since they left their winter base for the polar trek on 29 October.

It happened last Sunday, three days after the team had restarted their journey after a 16-day stop to rest and build a supply depot. While struggling through an area of 6 ft 'sastrugi' (snow dunes), Burton fell through a thin snow bridge into the crevasse.

'His safety rope and harness saved him and we pulled him out,' radioed expedition leader Sir Ranulph Fiennes. 'His sledge had acted as an anchor for him but in doing so it had turned over

'Charlie was unhurt and cheerful. The crevasse was a bad one but the safety system had worked.'

Fiennes also reported: 'The skidoos and sledges are taking a terrible battering from the sastrugi but are standing up well.'

The next day the ice team cleared the sastrugi, which had slowed their pace considerably, and were also cheered by a rise in the temperature — to the minus 20's C !

The team have now travelled about 800 miles and are two-thirds of the way to the Pole. They hope to arrive at Christmas, spend a few days there and then press on to McMurdo Sound

## Funny Money

Last month in New York City, a 16-year-old bank robber was dashing down the street clutching a bag of stolen cash when it suddenly exploded, spewing tear gas and splattering the young bandit with red dye. Within minutes the bleary-eyed and brightly marked teen-ager was apprehended. His stickup had been foiled by a tiny package that one bank manager calls "the state of the art in bank security systems."

The anticrime packet consists of an electronic detonator, a tear-gas canister and dye, all packed together so tightly that they fit inside the carved-out center of a stack of bills. Bank tellers keep the funny money in their cash drawers and slip it into a robber's bag along with the other loot. An electronic beam at the bank doors trips the detonator as the money is carried outside, and the hidden package explodes within 20 sec.

Most of the devices, which are used mainly by big-city banks and suburban ones that are frequently held up, are made by the U.S. Currency Protection Corp. of Arizona and IRI Americas in Pennsylvania. The firms, though, are facing a rival system made by Scented Money Deterrent Co. of Atlanta. That device releases the odor of rotten eggs, leaving a pungent trail for police to follow.

# Scheme to store oil in plastic bags

From Robert Whymant
in Tokyo

Japanese experts are considering putting the country's mounting oil stockpile in huge polyester bags floating on the sea's surface.

The idea has been developed by researchers at Tokyo University and the Ministry of International Trade and Industry because of a shortage of suitable land for constructing steel tanks. In 1978 Japan began stockpiling oil in tankers anchored off its coast. There are now 20 tankers containing 1,153 million gallons of crude oil — roughly equivalent to seven days' consumption.

Japan's total stockpile is for 110 days and the Government wants to build it up to 140 days' consumption, which is the average level of West European nations and the United States.

Because Japan is earthquake prone, steel tanks on land are expensive to construct, and suitable sites are hard to find.

According to the stockpile research team, polyester bags, about six millimetres thick, are cheaper, and would absorb earthquake shocks better than land tanks. The surface of the bags would be coated with polychloroprene (neoprene rubber) and the interior with nitrate butadiene rubber, and have a life of 20 years. Experiments are now in progress

If the researchers are satisfied, they will put their proposal to the Government and, if it is accepted, huge bags of oil will be seen bobbing on the waves offff Japan's coastline.

The stockpile research team points out one obvious danger — that of a ship colliding with the floating oil bags and puncturing them.

# Britons saved from island

From George Coats in Athens

THREE BRITONS were rescued from an uninhabited Greek island after clinging to a rock after their ship sank in a storm.

The three, identified by the port authorities as John Walker, aged 69, captain of the American-registered Wind Isle Princess, Neil Oldham, Janet Stones, 23, and Barbara Zimmer, 24, an American, were lifted from one of the Strofades islands some 30 miles south of Zakynthos by a Greek rescue helicopter.

# Dinosaur theory

From AP in Miami

A seven-mile wide chunk of rock and metal that crashed into the ocean 65 million years ago created enough energy to increase temperatures on earth rapidly and to wipe out the dinosaurs, a University of Miami scientist says. Cesare Emiliani, chairman of the university's geology department, advanced the theory in an article in the June issue of Eos magazine.

Mr Emiliani says the earth "became like a sauna bath and the dinosaurs could not get rid of the water from their bodies" fast enough

The rapid increase in temperatures also wiped out whole species of plants and animals.

## In the money

The first day of Harrods sale yesterday broke all records by taking more than £5 million. Earlier in the day security staff at the Knightsbridge store were called when scuffles broke out over half-price televisions.

# Italians bottom in trust poll

From Rory Watson
in Brussels

ITALIANS have emerged with the unenviable reputation of being the most distrustful and least trusted members of the European Community, in a new public opinion survey.

Two Italians in five have either no, or very little, confidence in their fellow countrymen, while fewer than one inhabitant in two from the other nine EEC countries would put their faith in an Italian, according to the survey, just published by the European Commission in Brussels.

The four countries at the foot of the trust poll are Italy, Greece, France and Ireland.

The Danes, Luxembourgers, Dutch and Belgians, command the most trust, with Germany and Britain sandwiched between. The north-south split is even more marked, and bodes ill for the EEC's further enlargement, when opinions are asked on the prospective members, Portugal and Spain.

The Portuguese come off particularly badly; fewer than three out of 10 EEC nationals trust them — with the greatest opposition coming from Luxembourg where there is already a large immigrant Portuguese population.

Looking outside its own frontiers, the Community continues to place great faith in both the Swiss and Americans, and increasingly the Chinese, but the standing of the Russians has deteriorated with fewer than 20 per cent prepared to trust them.

Even more worrying for France, which faces a presidential election this spring, and Greece, which holds elections for the national and European parliaments before the end of the year, is the strength of feeling against their existing societies.

One in 10 in each country would be prepared to " radically change the whole organisation of society by a revolutionary action."

Britain, predictably, continues to emerge as the greatest opponent of the EEC, with 50 per cent of the population considering it " a bad thing." Surprisingly, one of the EEC's other main critics is Ireland, which has received undeniable benefits since joining. One in four now oppose membership.

51

# The Bridge

## Description

There is a plan to replace the chain ferry across the mouth of Meryton Harbour with a suspension bridge. The participants are given roles to play which represent different attitudes to the plan. These roles are divided into four groups:

Group A: councillors, contractors and hoteliers
Group B: environmentalists and conservationists
Group C: ferry owner and ferry crew
Group D: members of the general public

The members of groups A, B and C have to persuade the members of group D to speak and vote on their side at the public meeting at the end of the simulation.

Before the simulation, there are newspaper articles and some facts and figures for the participants to read. A news broadcast sets the scene for the actual start of the simulation. This simulation is fairly straightforward and similar to the *Anglebury* simulation in its format. The only complicated factor is the arrangement of participants for the first hour or so of the simulation and this is explained fully below.

The simulation gives the participants a great deal of practice in explaining and justifying their points of view and persuading others to share them.

## Assigning roles and arranging groups

*The Bridge* simulation can be done with between 10 and 30 participants. As you've probably got some number between these extremes, the list below uses symbols to distinguish the more important from the less important roles:

the 10 '4-star roles' ★★★★ are essential
the  3 '3-star roles'  ★★★ are important
the  3 '2-star roles'   ★★ are quite important
the  6 '1-star roles'    ★ are very useful if there are enough participants
the  8 unstarred roles     can be left out if there aren't enough participants

| Group A<br>COUNCILLORS | Group B<br>NATURE RESERVE | Group C<br>FERRY OWNER | Group D<br>MEMBERS OF<br>THE PUBLIC |
|---|---|---|---|
| ★★★★Canford<br>★★Upton<br>★Talbot<br>Parley | ★★★★Sparrowe<br>★Hare<br>★Deere<br>Swift | ★★★★Hornblower<br><br>FERRY CREW<br><br>★★★★Heath<br>★Nelson<br>Chichester<br><br>(maximum: 4<br>minimum: 2) | ★★★★Smith<br>★★★★Brown<br>★★★★Robinson<br>★★★Jones<br>★★★White<br>★★★Davis<br>Williams<br>Roberts<br><br>(maximum: 8<br>minimum: 3) |
| CONTRACTORS<br><br>★★★★Macintosh<br>★★O'Hara<br>★Burns<br>O'Brien | ENVIRONMENTALISTS<br><br>★★★★Field<br>★Forest<br>Woods<br><br>(maximum: 7<br>minimum: 2) | | |
| HOTELIERS<br><br>★★★★Walker<br>★★Standing<br>Driver<br><br>(maximum: 11<br>minimum: 3) | | | |

In assigning roles, try to match the interests and opinions of the participants to the roles they'll be playing. The talking points discussion will help you to find out any strongly-held opinions among the participants.

Since the odds are slightly stacked against the pro-bridge lobby, make sure that there are some strong personalities in Group A. Apart from this, make sure each group has a good balance of ages, sexes, abilities and personalities.

## Organizing time

*Preparation*   The talking points, useful language and practice activities take about 45 minutes, longer if your students find the language unfamiliar and the practice activities provocative.

*The simulation*   The simulation itself needs a period of 3 to 4 hours, with an optional break about an hour before the end. If you only have 2 hours available, then the public meeting ('Scene Three') could perhaps take place another day. Ideally, though, there should be no such break in involvement. Fewer participants generally need less time, so a group of 10 to 15 participants could do the whole simulation in 1½ to 2 hours.

The simulation is in three 'scenes':

*Scene 1:* The members of the public hear the views of groups A, B and C in turn (in all 30 to 60 minutes)
*Scene 2:* Each group meets on its 'home territory' to plan its strategy for the public meeting (20 to 30 minutes)
*Scene 3:* All the participants attend the public meeting (60 to 90 minutes, depending on the number of participants)

In this specimen timetable the simulation is fitted into 3½ hours:

9.00  Give out role information.
9.15  Scene One begins – members of Group D move on every 20 minutes.
10.15  Scene Two begins.
10.45  End of Scene Two – coffee break.
11.00  Scene Three (public meeting) begins.
12.25  Vote taken, result announced.
12.30  End of simulation; written work set.

In this specimen timetable a smallish group of participants do the whole simulation in 1½ hours:

19.00  Give out role information.
19.10  Scene One begins – members of Group D move on every 10 minutes.
19.40  Scene Two begins.
20.00  Scene Three begins.
20.30  End of simulation; written work set.

*Follow-up*  The follow-up discussion takes 20 to 30 minutes, longer with a large number of participants with a lot of ideas.

## Arranging space

A large room divided into clearly identifiable areas is quite good enough for the simulation. If several rooms are available, however, it's worth using them in Scenes One and Two. It's very helpful to label each of the areas in Scenes One and Two, so that everyone knows exactly where they are supposed to be.

*SCENE ONE*

| SOUTH POINT Group A are here. | THE FERRY Group B are here. |

NORTH POINT Group C are here.

The members of the public (group D) are split into 3 sub-groups and play a sort of 'musical chairs':

Subgroup 1    start at South Point waiting for the ferry and listen to Group A's views for 15 to 20 minutes, then they get on the ferry and listen to Group B's views for 15 to 20 minutes, and finally, they get off the ferry at North Point and hear Group C's views for 15 to 20 minutes.

Subgroup 2    start on the ferry hearing Group B's views for 15 to 20 minutes, then get off the ferry at North Point and hear Group C's views for 15 to 20 minutes, and finally, go to South Point to hear Group A's views for another 15 to 20 minutes.

Subgroup 3    start at North Point hearing Group C, then go to South Point to hear Group A, and finally, wind up on the ferry to hear Group B.

*SCENE TWO*

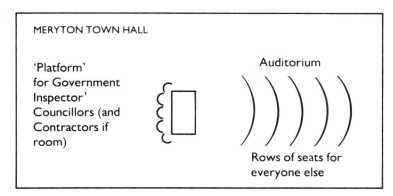

| THE GOLF CLUB | THE FERRY |
| Group A meet here. | Group B meet here. |

| THE NATURE RESERVE | THE GREY HERON INN |
| Group C meet here. | Group D meet here. |

Each of the four groups meets at its home base.

*SCENE THREE*

MERYTON TOWN HALL

'Platform' for Government Inspector' Councillors (and Contractors if room)

Auditorium

Rows of seats for everyone else

55

## What you need

Photocopies of the role information on pages 60 to 68, with
    participants' first names written in. Discard the role infor-
    mation for the roles you aren't using.
The *Eight Simulations* cassette and a cassette player for playing
    the 'Radio Meryton news broadcast'.
Your own timetable for the simulation and a list of the members
    of each group and their roles.
Cards to identify each of the areas in Scenes One and Two are
    also helpful : South Point, The Ferry etc.

## Preparation

*What the simulation is about*

1 Introduce the simulation to the class. Don't give too much
    information in case you spoil the surprise elements of the
    simulation.

*Talking points*

2 Perhaps put the students into groups to discuss the
    questions for a few minutes before beginning a general dis-
    cussion. Don't spend too long on this – the idea is simply to
    start the students talking about the topic, not to exhaust it!
3 A very advanced class may not need to spend long on the
    useful language and practice activities. It may be enough for
    them to just read through the useful language.

*Useful language*

4 Point out that arbitrary distinctions have been made in
    dividing up the expressions. For example, *Surely it depends
    on...* can be used to raise an objection and also to disagree
    and to present a counter-argument. In fact, these three
    functions overlap considerably. Make sure everyone can
    pronounce the expressions easily, by the way.
5 Get the students to suggest ways of finishing the incomplete
    sentences. For example:

    *Don't you agree that...      ...practice makes perfect?*

*Practice activities*

6 Divide the class into groups of three or four for the practice
    activities. Make sure everyone knows what they have to do
    before they start, as explained on pages 16 and 17 in the
    Participant's Book. Go round monitoring each group and
    offering corrections, praise and advice.
7 When most of the groups have finished the guided part of the
    practice, get them to think up their own points of view and
    present them to members of other groups. This can be done
    with the whole class reassembled, or everyone can stand up

and the members of each group can disperse round the class presenting their opinions to anyone they meet. This kind of free-for-all can be noisy but enjoyable.

*Before the simulation begins*

8   Make sure everyone reads the information on pages 18 to 21 in the Participant's Book before they come to the simulation. If necessary, run through any vocabulary you think your participants may find troublesome. Point out that the information *must* be read through carefully before the simulation day.

## The simulation

1   Prepare the room(s) and arrange the three areas for Scene One. For the time being the participants can sit where they like.

2   Give each participant his or her role information (photo-copied from pages 60 to 68 with real first names added). Allow a few minutes for reading and questions. Make sure everyone knows what they have to do.

3   Play the 'Radio Meryton news broadcast' on the cassette to the assembled participants. Here is a transcript:

'This is Radio Meryton news on the hour...

First, the latest development in the controversial plan to build a bridge across Meryton Harbour. There is to be a public meeting tonight at 8 p.m. to allow all parties to express their views. The leaders of the campaign against the bridge will be focussing their efforts on travellers across the ferry this morning. They intend to get as many members of the public as possible to attend tonight's meeting and vote against the scheme. At the same time campaigners in favour of the scheme will also be canvassing members of the public travelling on the ferry this morning. So it looks like an interesting morning on the North Point ferry and on the approach roads to it from the east and the west today. And tonight's public meeting in the Town Hall in Meryton looks as if it may produce a vote which will finally decide the future for the North Point ferry, which celebrated its 50th anniversary in 1978.

And now some news for farmers...'

*SCENE ONE*

4   Send Groups A, B and C to their areas (South Point, the ferry and North Point). Allow them a few minutes to 'plan their campaign'. Split up the 'members of the public' (Group D) into three sub-groups.

5   Sub-group 1 goes to South Point, sub-group 2 goes to the ferry and sub-group 3 goes to North Point. If you wish to monitor each group, don't interrupt or correct anyone. Make notes, perhaps.

6 After 15 to 20 minutes, blow a whistle or shout 'all change' and send Sub-group 1 to the ferry, Sub-group 2 to North Point and Sub-group 3 to South Point. Monitor as unobtrusively as possible.

7 After another 15 to 20 minutes, all change again and Sub-group 1 goes to North Point, Sub-group 2 to South Point and Sub-group 3 to the ferry. Monitor without interfering.

8 After another 15 to 20 minutes, stop everyone and create an extra area for Group D. The ferry keeps its title, Group A's area is relabelled 'Golf Club', Group C's area is relabelled 'Nature Reserve' and Group D's new area is labelled 'Grey Heron Inn'. Make sure everyone is now in their home area.

SCENE TWO

9 Each group holds a meeting on its home territory and discusses its success in the campaign so far and how it is going to approach the public meeting later. Go round to each group, listening in but not participating. Make notes on any language points you wish to mention at the follow-up discussion. Any militant groups who seem to be running out of things to say could compose leaflets, make placards or prepare posters.

SCENE THREE

10 After about 30 minutes, stop the group meetings. Allow the participants a short break while the seating is rearranged for the public meeting. The chairs should be arranged to represent the 'platform' where the councillors sit, and the 'auditorium' where everyone else sits. With a small number of participants, the contractors can share the platform.

The chair can be taken by the most responsible student among the councillors, or by you (as 'Lord Mayor' or as 'Government Inspector'), or best of all by another teacher who has been uninvolved so far (as 'Government Inspector'). Whoever is in the chair must make sure that every individual who wants to speak can and that each group is asked to sum up its point of view before the meeting closes.

11 Begin the public meeting. If you aren't in the chair yourself, make notes on language points to raise at the follow-up discussion. If a councillor is in the chair, be prepared to step in to take over if the meeting becomes unruly.

12 After 40 to 90 minutes (less with under 15 participants), everyone votes for or against the scheme. The results are declared and the simulation is over.

13 Set the written work. Allow the participants to choose their task or suggest one to them. Make sure everyone knows how long their work is to be and understands what they have to do.

14 Make sure everyone gives some thought to the questions for

58

the follow-up discussion before your next lesson together.

15 Just in case the 'public meeting' only lasts half an hour or so, it's worth being prepared to stop the simulation early, take a short break and have the follow-up discussion immediately afterwards.

## Follow-up

1 Preliminary small group discussions may be a good way to get things started – especially if no one has thought about the questions yet.

2 Find out what everyone thinks about the questions. What difficulties did they have? Have they any knowledge of similar real-life situations to the one in the simulation?

3 Point out any language points you made a note of during the simulation. Suggest remedial work.

4 If you haven't set the written work yet, set it now.

**CANFORD** – councillor

*You are a Conservative councillor and chairman of the Roads and Bridges Committee. You believe that the bridge should be built. You are absolutely sure that Collins and Sons' plan is a good one. You have promised your golfing partner, Macintosh, that you will make sure the plans are approved.*

*You need public support because there has been a lot of publicity about the scheme and suggestions of dishonesty and collusion have been made – unjustified, of course.*

Persuade the members of the public to support the plan.

---

**UPTON** – councillor

*You are a Liberal councillor and a member of the Roads and Bridges Committee. You support the plan to build a bridge because it will bring tourists and jobs to the area. You are not totally convinced that Collins and Sons' plan and their price are the best, even though Councillor Canford supports them. You believe the bridge should be free for all users and not a toll bridge.*

*You need public support for the idea of the bridge, though not necessarily for Collins and Sons' design.*

Persuade the members of the public to support the plan.

---

**TALBOT** – councillor

*You are a Conservative councillor and deputy chairman of the Roads and Bridges Committee. You believe that the design and concept of the new bridge is a wonderful forward-looking idea. It will be much cheaper to build it now than to wait for a few years.*

*You need public support because there have been many letters in the papers from people who are against the scheme.*

Persuade the members of the public to support the plan.

**PARLEY** – councillor

*You are a Labour councillor and a member of the Roads and Bridges Committee. You believe that the bridge will improve communications in the area, but you think it could be built more cheaply than by Collins and Sons.*

*You need public support for the idea of the bridge.*

Persuade the members of the public to support the plan.

**MACINTOSH** – contractor

*You are the chairman of Collins and Sons, the civil engineering contractors. Your plans for building the bridge will lift your company out of a financial crisis. Councillor Canford is your golfing partner and he has promised to make sure your offer is accepted. In return you will build him a new house very cheaply.*

*There have been a lot of protests about the bridge from fanatics like bird-watchers and nature-lovers. The public needs to be made aware of how vital the bridge would be to the economy of the area.*

Persuade the members of the public to support the plan.

**O'HARA** – contractor

*You are the chief engineer of Collins and Sons, the civil engineering contractors. Your staff have prepared the designs and the techniques to be used are revolutionary and very exciting because of the need to allow shipping to pass under the bridge. The price your company is quoting is realistic.*

*There have been a lot of protests against the bridge. If it is built, you could become really famous as a brilliant bridge designer.*

Persuade the members of the public to support the plan.

**BURNS** – contractor

*You are the managing director of Collins and Sons, the civil engineering contractors. You believe the design of the bridge is superb and that the price is realistic. You have spent a lot of money doing research and preparing plans, so it is important that the bridge is built to repay this expenditure.*

*There has been a lot of opposition to the scheme in the press.*

Persuade the members of the public to support the plan.

**O'BRIEN** – contractor

*You are a site engineer for Collins and Sons, the civil engineering contractors. You have helped with the practical side of the plans and you believe they are excellent. Building the bridge would bring you to the South of England to work. This is preferable to the North of Scotland, where you would have to work otherwise.*

*There has been a lot of anti-bridge propaganda in the papers recently.*

Persuade the members of the public to support the plan.

**WALKER** – hotelier

*You are the owner of the Hotel Majestic in Meryton. You support the plan to build a bridge because your guests are always complaining about the long delays at the ferry in the summer. If the bridge was free, not a toll bridge, more visitors would come to Meryton and this would make your hotel busier.*

*There has been a lot of opposition from idiots like naturalists and left-wing so-called environmentalists.*

Persuade the members of the public to support the plan.

---

### STANDING – hotelier

*You are the owner of the Hotel Romantica in Meryton. The proposed bridge will attract more holiday-makers to Meryton and improve road communications. Many of your guests drive to Netherfield and Longbourne-on-Sea for day trips and arrive back at your hotel angry about the delays at the ferry.*

*There have been a lot of objections to the proposal. You can see the objectors' point of view but your hotel's profitability is at stake.*

Persuade the members of the public to support the plan.

---

### DRIVER – hotelier

*You are the owner of the Hotel Bellavista in Longbourne-on-Sea. The proposed bridge will be an important attraction for visitors to your hotel. At present they are cut off from the entertainments of nearby Meryton, because the ferry stops running before midnight, even in the summer. You believe the bridge should be free and not a toll bridge.*

*A lot of local people in Longbourne are opposed to the idea of the bridge.*

Persuade the members of the public to support the plan.

---

### HORNBLOWER – ferry owner

*You are the owner of the North Point Floating Bridge ferry. Your family has been running ferries across Meryton Harbour for generations. If they build a bridge, the ferry will stop running and your 12 employees will lose their jobs. You will lose your source of income and you expect to be compensated for this. Nonetheless, you are totally opposed to the idea of building the bridge.*

Persuade the members of the public to oppose the plan.

**HEATH** – ferry crew member

*You are the captain of the North Point Floating Bridge ferry. If they build the bridge you will become unemployed. You know that people enjoy travelling on the ferry, and a modern bridge would not provide the same pleasurable experience.*

Persuade the members of the public to oppose the plan.

**NELSON** – ferry crew member

*You work on the North Point ferry. If they build the bridge you will lose your job – though there is a chance you might be re-employed as a toll-collector. You believe the old-fashioned ways are the best.*

Your employer has asked you to explain to the passengers on the ferry today why they should oppose the plan to build a bridge.

**CHICHESTER** – ferry crew member

*You work on the ferry between South Point and North Point. If they build the bridge, you would lose your job. There is a chance that you might be re-employed as a toll-collector for a few years, but this would not be a secure job with a pension. You are against the scheme.*

Your employer has asked you to persuade the passengers on the ferry today to oppose the plan to build a bridge.

**SPARROWE** – Nature reserve

*You are the administrator of the Netherfield Heath Nature Reserve. The building of the bridge would have a catastrophic effect on wildlife. Pollution and people would drive away many wild animals and rare birds.*

Persuade the members of the public to oppose the plan.

**HARE** – Nature reserve

*You are a warden at the Netherfield Heath Nature Reserve. Building the bridge would put an end to your hopes of establishing a breeding colony of Deptford warblers. North Point would become just an extension of the urban sprawl of Meryton.*

Persuade the members of the public to oppose the plan.

**DEERE** – Nature reserve

*You are a voluntary unpaid warden at the Netherfield Heath Nature Reserve. You are against the building of the bridge because it would mean the end of the nature reserve as you know it. Meryton is very fortunate to have such an unspoilt piece of countryside on its doorstep.*

Persuade the members of the public to oppose the plan.

**SWIFT** – Nature reserve

*You are a warden at the Netherfield Heath Nature Reserve. It is already very difficult to protect the wildlife in the reserve from ignorant holiday-makers and children from Meryton. If a bridge was built, it would be impossible.*

Persuade the members of the public to oppose the plan.

**FIELD** – environmentalist

*You are the secretary of the local Friends of the Earth. You believe that if they built a bridge, there would be an intolerable amount of pollution in and around Meryton Harbour, which is already threatened by the oil-wells near Westleton.*

Persuade the members of the public to oppose the plan.

**FOREST** – environmentalist

*You are the local secretary of the Ramblers Association, representing the interests of country walkers. You believe that Netherfield Heath is threatened by the proposal to build a bridge. At the moment it is still unspoilt and an ideal place for walkers and bird-watchers.*

Persuade the members of the public to oppose the plan.

**WOODS** – environmentalist

*You are the local representative of the Countryside Commission, an organization which aims to preserve rural England. The building of a bridge would bring thousands of day-trippers into a protected area and probably destroy the balance of nature there.*

Persuade the members of the public to oppose the plan.

**SMITH**

*You live in Longbourne-on-Sea and teach at a school in Meryton. You drive to and from work. The proposed bridge would make your journey time much shorter, especially in the summer. It would enable you to make the journey in about half an hour.*

**BROWN**

*You live in Longbourne-on-Sea and work in Meryton in a bank. You always take the bus to North Point, catch the ferry and catch another bus into Meryton. There is a direct bus to Meryton, but you enjoy the sea-trip on deck on the ferry. If they built a bridge, the bus service would be faster. More people would come to Longbourne, which is pleasantly quiet outside the holiday season.*

**ROBINSON**

*You drive the bus from Longbourne-on-Sea to Meryton. You enjoy your job because there are not too many passengers and it's a pleasant drive. If they built a bridge there would be many more passengers and there would be a lot more heavy traffic on the narrow road through Netherfield. Your bus has priority on the ferry, so you don't have to join the queues of cars in the summer.*

**JONES**

*You live in Netherfield and you own the pub there, the Grey Heron Inn. The proposed bridge would bring more customers, but in the summer you are busy enough anyway. You appreciate the sleepiness of the village.*

**WHITE**

*You live in Meryton. Every weekend you go to South Point, take the ferry and go for a walk on the other side. The proposed bridge would bring thousands of people in their cars to North Point and Netherfield.*

## DAVIS

*You live and work in Netherfield village. If they built a bridge, the village would be more lively. It would be easier to get to the shops and cinemas in Meryton.*

## WILLIAMS

*You own the shop at South Point. The proposed bridge would take away most of your customers, who buy things from your shop while they are waiting for the ferry.*

## ROBERTS

*You live at South Point. There is a lot of traffic in the summer outside your house and this is annoying. If they built a bridge, perhaps this would take the traffic away to the other side of the harbour.*

# The Language Centre

## Description

This simulation is in two distinct halves which can be separated by a break of between ten minutes and ten days. Each half consists of committee meetings, informal consultation sessions and a plenary meeting. The participants are assigned to one of five committees, each of which discusses different aspects of the organization of a language school.

In this simulation all the basic information the participants need is in the Participant's Book. The only extra information they need is their role, the points on the agenda their committee should concentrate on and the deadlines. The Controller gives this information at the beginning of each half.

The aims are to provoke discussion about a topic most students are experts on – learning English, and to provide an insight into the way a relatively complex organization works.

## Assigning roles and arranging groups

There are five committees, made up as follows:

| Group A ADMINISTRATION | Group B TEACHERS OF ADVANCED STUDENTS | Group C TEACHERS OF ELEMENTARY STUDENTS | Group D ADVANCED STUDENTS | Group E ELEMENTARY STUDENTS |
|---|---|---|---|---|
| 3 to 6 members | | | | |
| Director of Studies Head of Advanced Dept. Head of Elementary Dept. | 3 to 6 teachers | 3 to 6 teachers | 3 to 6 students | 3 to 6 students |
| (A deputy for each may be appointed if required.) | | | | |

With fewer than fifteen participants you may decide to have committees of two in each if all your participants enjoy discussions and have plenty of ideas. If this is not the case, it is better to combine the two Students' committees and perhaps also combine the two Teachers' committees. With more than fifteen students this is not desirable.

Each committee should be roughly the same size. So, with twenty participants, the Administration committee might consist of the Director of Studies, the Deputy Director of Studies and the two Heads of Department; the other committees would have four members each.

In the consultation sessions, there are some extra roles: Professors of Education – these are to be played by you and any other teachers you can round up. Their role is simply to answer questions on language teaching, advise on teaching methods and textbooks and all in all to provide any professional knowledge which the participants themselves need to help them in their deliberations.

In assigning roles, try to make sure that the participants aren't given roles they might find unpleasant or embarrassing. For example, the weakest students in the class shouldn't be made members of the Elementary Students committee, in case they feel insulted. (Particularly sensitive participants may need reminding that they are supposed to be expressing the points of view of the different groups in the school and that they haven't been given roles to match their level of English.) Otherwise, try to make sure that each group is well balanced in terms of ages, sexes, personalities and abilities. If the Director of Studies or the Deputy Director of Studies is going to chair the plenary meetings, they need to be participants who are capable of doing this fairly and sensibly – and they may need careful individual briefing before the simulation begins.

It might be a good idea to redistribute roles in the second half of the simulation if any groups have not been working harmoniously or if a change would liven them up. This redistribution can be planned ahead or worked out just before the second half starts. A change of role can be stimulating but if everyone has settled into their committees and is working well, it's probably best to let them stay as they are. Alternatively, just a few of the participants can swop roles.

In this simulation, particularly with a large number of participants, it is important for each participant to have a badge or label to wear, so that he or she can be easily identified by others. The badge would show the role the participant is playing, like this:

|  |  |  |
|---|---|---|
| MARIA<br>Teacher of advanced<br>students | or | PETER<br>Deputy Director<br>of Studies |

Sticky labels are cheap and can easily be stuck to clothing without marking it permanently. Pin-on badges can be re-used.

## Organizing time and arranging space

*Preparation*     The talking points, useful language and practice activities take about 45 minutes.

*The simulation*     The simulation is in two halves with a break in between. This break could be a tea-break, a lunch break or even a break of a day or several days. This would depend on your own timetable, of course. Each half takes 1½ to 2 hours, making 3 to 4 hours in all.

This specimen timetable fits the whole simulation into 3¾ hours:

9.00  Start read-in of Part One.
9.15  Finish read-in, start committee meetings.
9.45  Begin consultation between groups.
10.05  Begin plenary meeting in one room.
10.40  Finish plenary meeting. (Coffee break)     *End of Part One.*
11.00  Start read-in of Part Two.
11.10  Begin committee meetings.
11.40  Begin consultation session.
12.05  Begin plenary meeting.
12.45  Finish plenary meeting.     *End of Part Two.*
     Set written work.

On pages 28 and 30 of the Participant's Book, there are two programmes with gaps ( ......... ) for the deadlines to be filled in. These deadlines are the times by which each of the meetings must be finished. Since all five committees will be working towards the same deadlines, it's important that the deadlines are adhered to by everyone. Your deadlines will depend on your own timetable, of course, but here is an indication of how long each meeting should be:

PART ONE

1 Read-in 15 to 20 minutes
2 Committee meetings 30 to 35 minutes
3 Consultation 15 to 25 minutes
4 Plenary meeting 30 to 40 minutes

Total: 90 to 120 minutes

PART TWO

1 Read-in 10 minutes
2 Committee meetings 30 to 35 minutes
3 Consultation 20 to 30 minutes
4 Plenary meeting 30 to 45 minutes

Total: 90 to 120 minutes

Each of the five committees needs a separate area to hold their meeting in. These could be five areas of one room but if you have two rooms available, the two Students' committees could meet in one room and the other three committees in the other. If three rooms are available, separate the Administration committee from the others. Try to arrange the furniture so that each committee has as much privacy as possible.

During the Consultation sessions everyone is free to go from area to area consulting members of other committees. Some participants would stay in their committee's area to receive visits from members of other committees. Some committees may decide to forgo some of their consultation time in order to continue their committee meetings, so don't arrange the seating for the plenary meeting too soon!

The plenary meeting takes place in one room, with the seating arranged to represent an assembly hall. The members of the Administration committee sit on the 'platform' and everyone else sits in the rows of seats facing them. The chair might be taken by one of the Administration committee, if they can be relied upon to allow everyone to have their say and to control the meeting fairly. If they can't, it might be better for you or another teacher to chair the meeting in the role of 'Principal'.

*Follow-up*     The follow-up discussion should be done after both halves of the simulation are over, preferably after a long break or the next day. The discussion might take 20 to 40 minutes – longer if a lot of remedial work seems necessary.

## What you need

(No photocopying is needed for this simulation.)

A prepared programme of deadlines for each half of the simulation. You will announce these at the beginning of each half.

A slip of paper for each participant with details of his or her role and the agenda items to concentrate on. The slips would look like this:

> MARIA - Teacher of advanced students
> Agenda items 1, 4 and 6

These are the agenda items for each committee:

|  | PART ONE | PART TWO |
|---|---|---|
| Director of Studies and Deputy... | 1, 5 & 7 | 2, 6 & 7 |
| Head of Advanced Dept and Deputy... | 1, 3 & 7 | 1, 2 & 7 |
| Head of Elementary Dept and Deputy... | 1, 5 & 7 | 1, 2 & 7 |
| Teachers of Advanced Students... | 1, 4 & 6 | 1, 3 & 5 |
| Teachers of Elementary Students... | 1, 4 & 3 | 1, 3 & 4 |
| Advanced Students... | 1, 2 & 6 | 1, 4 & 5 |
| Elementary Students... | 1, 2 & 5 | 1, 2 & 6 |

A badge or label for each participant (a blank label can be filled in by the participants themselves).
A badge or label for each of the Professors of Education.
Three copies each of some elementary textbooks for Part Two (if possible) and also: three copies each of some upper-intermediate or advanced textbooks (if possible). These will all be used in place of or in addition to the textbook blurbs on pages 26 and 27 of the Participant's Book. Using them will add a lot of realism to the first item on the agenda of Part Two.

## Preparation

*Talking points*
1  After introducing the simulation, discuss the talking points. Help the students with vocabulary.

*Useful language*
2  A very advanced class, or a class who have recently done *The Bridge* simulation, may not need to spend very long on this — just get them to read through the useful language section. Most classes will benefit from a revision and from the practice, too.

*Practice activities*
3  The practice activities suggested on page 25 of the Participant's Book will more readily come to life if the topics suggested are actually written on the board in your classroom. Further topics can then be added later.
     Follow the three phases suggested in the Participant's Book and go round to each group offering advice and corrections.

73

*Before the simulation begins*
4  Make sure everyone reads this section carefully. They will need time to sleep on points 3 and 4. It might be a good idea to run through any vocabulary you think may be troublesome in the two agendas.

## The simulation

PART ONE
1  Give everyone a slip of paper with their role and their committee's agenda items (see *What you need* above).
2  Announce the deadlines for Part One and make sure everyone makes a note of them in their books

read-in
3  Allow 15 to 20 minutes for the read-in. This is to give everyone time to prepare their views on the agenda items before they discuss them in committee.
4  Give everyone a badge or label. Make sure everyone understands what to do.
5  Arrange seating areas for the committee meetings.

committee meetings
6  The committee meetings begin. Each group is responsible for its own discussion, so don't interfere in any meeting. Under no circumstances should you put forward your own opinions while you are listening in to a committee.
7  Meanwhile, round up some other teachers to be Professors of Education. Give them each a badge and explain what they'll have to do: to answer questions on any items on the agenda and to offer advice when requested. If necessary, be a Professor of Education yourself.

consultation session
8  After 30 to 35 minutes (keeping strictly to your deadlines), the committees break up and the consultation session begins. Some participants will leave their committee's area to go and consult other committees, others will stay behind and be consulted. The Professors of Education should also be available for consultation during this session.

Some participants may need to be prompted to get up and move, so be prepared to step in and make sure the consultation does take place.
9  Some committees may decide to meet again briefly before the end of the consultation session to discuss what they have found out from the other committees. Encourage this if the consultation is losing its impetus.
10  Rearrange seating for the plenary meeting. If one of the participants is going to chair the meeting, brief him or her on what to do and what to say. Make sure he or she lets each committee make its recommendations.

**plenary meeting** 11 After 15 to 25 minutes' consultation (according to your deadline), the plenary meeting begins. The chair can be taken by one of the participants, or by yourself or by another teacher in the role of Principal.

The agenda should be gone through item by item, starting with item 1. Make sure the meeting doesn't get bogged down with an early item to the exclusion of all the later ones.

12 The deadline for the plenary meeting can be more flexible than the others. If the meeting is lively and everyone is contributing, you could run on into the break, for example, but this will depend, of course, on your timetable arrangements.

After 30 to 40 minutes, finish the plenary meeting.

13 This is the end of Part One. Take a break before Part Two. Or do Part Two another day.

14 Decide on any redistribution of roles for Part Two. If you are replacing an incompetent Director of Studies, for example, it may be prudent to reassign several other roles to disguise what is being done and spare the feelings of the participant who has 'failed'. Redistributing too many roles may, however, reduce the involvement the participants have built up in Part One.

15 Arrange the seating for five areas for Part Two.

**PART TWO read-in** 16 Give everyone a slip of paper with their role and their committee's agenda items. Send them to their committee's area to think about the agenda items.

17 Announce the deadlines for Part Two and make sure everyone makes a note of them in their books.

18 Give out the textbooks as follows:
Administration committee – one copy of each book
Teachers of advanced students – one copy of each upper-intermediate or advanced book
Teachers of elementary students – one copy of each elementary book
Advanced students – one copy of each upper-intermediate or advanced book
Elementary students – one copy of each elementary book
If you can't find enough textbooks to lend out, the blurbs on pages 26 and 27 of the Participant's Book can represent the textbooks.

**committee meetings** 19 After 10 minutes' read-in, the committee meetings begin. If you wish to monitor each group and make notes on language points to raise later, take care not to be tempted to participate in the meetings.

20 Meanwhile, round up some other teachers to be Professors of Education in the consultation session.

**consultation session**

21 After 30 to 35 minutes the committee meetings stop and the consultation session begins. Encourage inactive participants to go and find out what other committees have been discussing.

22 Rearrange seating for the plenary meeting. If a participant is to chair the meeting, brief him or her beforehand.

**plenary meeting**

23 After 20 to 30 minutes' consultation, the plenary meeting begins. The chair can be taken by the Director of Studies or the Deputy Director, by yourself or by another teacher in the role of Principal. Make sure the agenda is followed item by item and that each committee is allowed to present its recommendations.

24 The plenary meeting can be open-ended if your timetable allows. Otherwise stick to your deadline and close the meeting after 30 to 45 minutes. End of Part Two.

25 Set the written work. Ask everyone to consider the follow-up discussion questions.

## Follow-up

1 Find out what everyone thinks by asking the questions. Make your own comments on their communicative performance. Suggest any necessary remedial work.

2 Set the written work if you haven't already.

# People in the News

## Description

The participants are divided into two or three teams which work independently to prepare and record a radio (or TV) programme. Each team receives the same input of press releases, news items and telephoned reports but the content of each programme is geared to its 'audience': highbrow, middlebrow or lowbrow. If you have video available then the programmes can be television shows, but radio broadcasts using a tape recorder will be almost as interesting.

Each team works to a deadline and collects the news items from the Controller at the 'Newsroom' every 20 minutes during the preparation time. Using individual cassette recorders, each team can go 'on the air' simultaneously; or if the recording is to be done in a central 'studio', the deadlines are staggered to make sure each team is ready at the right time.

The aim of the simulation is to provide plenty of opportunity for the participants to work together in an English-speaking team under pressure, understand and evaluate a large number of written and spoken texts, and prepare and perform several interviews and news reports.

## Assigning roles and arranging groups

Each team should consist of no fewer than four and no more than ten. This means that if you have between ten and fourteen participants it's best to have only two EBC stations, leaving out EBC-3 perhaps.

Each team should be well-balanced: different abilities, personalities, nationalities and sexes. Each team needs a team-leader to be its 'Producer', whose job it is to co-ordinate the preparation of the programme. The Producer can be appointed by the Controller or elected by the team.

## Organizing time and arranging space

*Preparation*  The talking points, useful language and practice activities take about 45 minutes to cover.

77

*The simulation*   The whole simulation requires an uninterrupted period of 3 to 4 hours. A shortened version lasting 1½ to 2 hours can be arranged by not issuing all of the news items – but try not to do this randomly, because many earlier items are related to later ones. There should be no interruption of concentration for breaks. If refreshments are needed, arrange for these to be taken into the classroom. The programmes themselves should be 10 minutes long, although with only two teams, 15-minute programmes might be better if there's enough time.

In this specimen timetable the whole simulation is fitted into 3¾ hours, with staggered deadlines:

9.00   Each team goes to its room or area to discuss how to organize the work
9.10   Each team collects its first items
9.30   2nd batch of items collected
9.50   3rd batch collected
10.10  Cassettes of telephoned reports collected
10.30  4th batch collected
10.50  5th batch collected
11.10  EBC-1 collects its last batch and
       EBC 2 and 3 collect their 6th
11.30  EBC-1 starts its final rehearsal and
       EBC-2 collects its last batch and
       EBC-3 collects its last-but-one batch
11.50  EBC-1 goes to the studio and
       EBC-2 starts its final rehearsal and
       EBC-3 collects its last batch
12.10  EBC-1 takes a break and
       EBC-2 goes to the studio and
       EBC-3 starts its final rehearsal
12.30  EBC-2 takes a break and
       EBC-3 goes to the studio
12.45  EBC-3 finishes its recording and the simulation is over.

With simultaneous deadlines, the whole schedule looks much simpler, although for this to be done, each team has to be in a separate room with its own tape recorder.

Depending on the time available, the news items are divided into between four and ten batches for the teams to collect. They must be collected every 20 minutes even if a team isn't ready for them yet – that's a rule! (In a 1½ hour simulation this is reduced to every 15 minutes.) The cassette of telephoned reports is given to each team for 20 minutes only if you just have the one copy available, but if you have several copies of the cassette, then each team can have its own copy to keep for longer and listen to again later.

In this specimen timetable a shortened version of the simulation using about half of the news items and with each team having the same deadline takes only 1½ hours to complete:

19.00 Each team goes to its room or area and receives its first batch of news items.
19.15 Each team collects its second batch of items.
19.30 Cassettes of telephoned reports collected.
19.45 Third batch collected.
20.00 Last batch collected.
20.10 Rehearsals start.
20.20 Each team records its programme.
20.30 End of simulation, written work set.

Ideally, each team should have its own room to work in undisturbed, but failing this, one room divided into separate areas will serve. If you can get a large table for each team to sit round, it will help to create a good working atmosphere.

*Follow-up* The follow-up discussion lasting about 15 minutes should take
*and* place *before* the recordings are played back. Playing back the
*playback* recordings to everyone will take about 30 minutes, longer if you pause the tape frequently and ask for or make a lot of comments.

## What you need

Three photocopies each of pages 84 to 95. These should be cut up ready and stapled together in batches for each team. Keep the batches in separate piles and number each batch if your teams are working to staggered deadlines.
The cassette of five telephoned reports. If possible, copy the relevant section of the *Eight Simulations* cassette onto a blank cassette and make three copies so that each team can have its own.
A cassette recorder for each team with a blank cassette in, if possible. Or just one cassette player to be shared.
Your own schedule of deadlines and recording times.
A list of the members of each team.
If you're recording the programmes in a central 'studio', a tape recorder with a proper microphone is better than a built-in microphone. Or you can use video equipment if it's available.

## Preparation

*Talking points*

1 Introduce the simulation and discuss the talking points.
2 If the participants haven't done the *World News Magazine* simulation, there is some useful language on page 10 in the Participant's Book. Even if they have done this before, it might be worth doing a quick revision.

*Useful language*

3 Look at the linking techniques in this section.

*Practice activities*

4 To practise the linking techniques, the students should work things out in pairs before the class as a whole is involved.
5 Follow the suggestions on page 34 in the Participant's Book to practise improvising interviews.

*Before the simulation begins*

6 Make sure everyone reads the texts on pages 35 to 37 of their books before they come to the simulation.

## The simulation

1 Tell the participants which team they're in and show them which area or room to go to.
2 Allow each team 10 to 15 minutes to organize themselves and elect a team-leader (unless you decide to nominate one). They should also agree on their station's policy, bearing in mind the statements on page 36 and the letters on pages 36-7 of the Participant's Book. Make sure everyone knows what they have to do.
3 Announce to each team its deadline and the times when they have to collect the latest news from you in the 'Newsroom'. Point out that the news items will be available every 20 minutes and that they *must* be collected every 20 minutes. If necessary, write up the collection times on the board.
4 Go back to the 'Newsroom' with a member of each team and give them their first batch of press releases and news items.
5 Continue issuing news items every 20 minutes. If a team is late collecting, send them a reminder on a slip of paper. Like this, perhaps:

> To: EBC-2 *People in the News*
> From: Controller, EBC Newsroom
> A batch of five news items is awaiting your collection

6  After two or three batches of news items have been collected, the telephoned reports on the cassette can be collected. If you have only one copy, each team may keep it for 20 minutes only before returning it to you. After that, they collect their next batch of news items and the cassette is given to the next team for 20 minutes. Here is a transcript of the 5 reports:

'This is John Forster, reporting from Plymouth.

There's still no news of the whereabouts of the transatlantic sailor, Mr Jim Cook, who has been missing since Sunday. His last reported position is 250 kilometres west of Land's End.

The last few days have been marked by storms of unprecedented ferocity. Hurricane force winds have been battering the Cornish coast and even the largest ships have been putting into port to shelter from the storm. Mr Cook, who set out from Brazil 6 weeks ago to sail single-handed to England, seemed to be making good time until the storms hit the Western Approaches on Sunday. He was making regular radio reports to the Post Office Radio Station here in Plymouth. These reports stopped on Saturday and there is now great concern for Mr Cook's safety. Local fisherman, Joe Watts, told me that in seas like these no-one could survive and other local people seem to share this view. RAF rescue planes have been grounded so far this week because of the storms and so any attempt by the authorities to trace Mr Cook's yacht will have to wait until there is an improvement in the weather. In the meantime, all his wife, Doreen, and 12-year-old daughter, Sarah, can do is sit and wait and hope for a miracle.

It doesn't look very likely that Mr Cook is going to be found alive. With that gloomy prediction, this is John Forster signing off.'

'This is Richard Denman in Buenos Aires.

After a stunning first half, England were leading Argentina by 6 goals to nil. The Argentinian defence were really at sixes and sevens: Mistake after mistake by Rodriguez and Schmidt gave the England strikers more chances than they knew how to cope with. It could have been 20-0 by half time if Greenfield had been on his usual form, but as it was the 6 goals were scored by Robinson (4) and Taylor (2). Taylor's 2nd goal, scored just 30 seconds before the half-time whistle, was an amazing flying header which left Argentinian goalkeeper, Morales, sitting shaking his head on his goal line.

When play re-started after half time, England's goal bonanza seemed to be over. The Argentinian manager had substituted reserve goalkeeper, Gomez, for the unlucky Morales and his influence seemed to tighten up the defence and stop them making the mistakes which cost them so dearly in the first half. Still, England retained possession most of the time but 20 minutes before the end, a mistake by Greenfield gave Alvarez the ball and with an open goal, Garcia made it 6-1.

Suddenly, Alvarez and Garcia came to life and with the support of Carlos, a series of brilliant moves left the England defence nowhere as they made the score 2-6, 3-6, 4-6, 5-6! With only 2 minutes to go the Argentinian crowd were going wild! But now the time had come for England's luck to change and a bad pass by Carlos went to Taylor who raced up the field to beat goalkeeper, Gomez, with a 30-

metre pile-driver into the corner of the net. With the score now 7-5, England's victory seemed secure, but Alvarez and Garcia worked their magic again to make it 7-6. With only ten seconds to go, Jackson very crudely and stupidly brought down Carlos in the penalty area. Alvarez took the penalty and as the final whistle went drove the ball into the back of the net, making the final score 7 all.

A fantastic game. Full of surprises and a tremendous demonstration of the skills of these 2 brilliant teams. Man of the match undoubtedly was Alvarez, who scored 5 of the 7 Argentinian goals. Next month's return match at Wembley is clearly not to be missed. So there we are, 7 goals each and a memorable match. This is Richard Denman in Buenos Aires.'

 'This is Michael Roberts in Paris.

News is just coming in of another kidnapping in the South of France. The family of the millionaire French industrialist, M. Jean Rabelais, are being held by the kidnappers and a £1 million ransom is being demanded.

The kidnapping happened late last night when M. Rabelais and his family were dining at a restaurant in the town of Cagnes-sur-mer on the French Riviera. M. Rabelais himself was released soon after to raise the ransom money, but his wife, Marie, and his two sons, Jean-Marc and Jean-Francois are still being held in a secret hiding place. The kidnappers are demanding £1 million by midnight tonight and are threatening to kill their hostages if the money is not paid. The police have made it clear that M. Rabelais should not pay the kidnappers the money. They fear that if he gives in to their demands, a whole series of similar kidnappings will follow. M. Rabelais refuses to talk to the press, but it is understood that he is under strong pressure from the police to play for time and refuse to pay the ransom. This is Michael Roberts in Paris.'

 'This is Sue Clarke, outside the Broadcasting Union Headquarters in London. Meetings have been going on here all day between the employers and Union leaders to try to bring to an end the dispute between them. Unless a settlement can be reached before lunchtime today, it looks as if all television and radio will be off the air this evening. Mr Bill Lord, General Secretary of the Union, told me just now: "My members have been underpaid for 2 years at least. It's time the employers realized that my members have had enough of being taken for a ride like this. They work long and unsocial hours and they deserve a fair wage for the amount of responsibility they have. If we can't reach an agreement by today noon, I'll bring my members out on strike with effect from 6 o'clock tonight and that's official."

So there we are. Things look pretty grim and it looks as if TV and radio really will be off the air tonight. This is Sue Clarke outside the Broadcasting Union Headquarters.'

 'This is John Forster again from Plymouth.

Fantastic news! The lone transatlantic sailor, Jim Cook, is just sailing into Plymouth Harbour! His yacht has a badly torn sail but otherwise seems undamaged. He was first spotted just 20 minutes ago and there's already an enormous crowd here on the quayside to welcome him. He looks well but very tired, he probably hasn't slept for several days. He was smiling and waving to everyone just now and he really looks in great shape.

His wife and daughter are here on the quayside and in a couple of minutes Mr Cook should be here on dry land. This really is a terribly moving occasion – women in the crowd are crying with relief.

Local people said it would be a miracle if he came through these storms alive and he has. It's absolutely unbelievable, but it's true. Jim Cook is alive, I can see him now...he's waving again to the people on the quay and...yes...he's spotted his wife up there and he's blowing her a kiss.

This is an amazing experience! This is John Forster here in Plymouth.'

7 Between collection times, you as Controller will have time to go from group to group listening in and making notes on language points. Don't butt in while the teams are working. But if someone asks you to check their spelling, for example, it would be unkind to refuse.

8 When the recording times are approaching, make sure each team spends time on a final rehearsal for their programme. About 20 minutes before the deadline should be set aside for this.

9 [If each team has its own tape recorder and is working in a separate room, the deadlines can all be the same. Make sure, before they start recording, that the equipment works by doing a short test recording. Make sure each team knows when to start and when to finish. There is no need for you to be present if the teams know how to operate their recorders.

At the end of the recordings, collect up the cassettes, announce when they'll be played back and set the written work. End of the simulation.]

With staggered deadlines and each team recording in a central 'studio' (another room): the news items in each batch will have been arranged so that the first team to go to the studio have received all their items in time. Then 20 minutes before EBC-1's deadline, EBC-1 begins its final rehearsal, EBC-2 receives its last items and EBC-3 receives its penultimate items.

10 20 minutes later, EBC-1 records its programme, EBC-2 starts its rehearsal and EBC-3 receives its last items.

11 20 minutes later, EBC-1 finishes recording and takes a break, EBC-2 records its programme and EBC-3 starts its rehearsal.

12 20 minutes later, EBC-2 finishes recording and takes a break and EBC-3 records its programme.

13 10 to 20 minutes later EBC-3 finishes its recording.

14 Reassemble the participants to announce when the recordings will be played back. Set the written work.
(Or do this after each team finishes its recording.)

## Follow-up

1 Start the follow-up discussion *before* playing back the recordings. This will help the participants to concentrate on talking about the preparation for the programme, rather than just the programme itself and its impact.
2 Find out everyone's answers to the questions and make your own comments on their communicative performance. Give praise as well as criticism.
3 Play back the recordings. Perhaps pause after each interview or report for comments, or simply play each programme right through and ask for comments afterwards. Don't criticize faults in broadcasting technique – the participants aren't professionals.
4 Perhaps round everything off by coming back to some of the questions you discussed earlier.
5 Set the written work, if you haven't already.

MISS EBC

The annual Miss EBC contest will take place at the end of next month.

If you're attractive, intelligent and unmarried, then you're eligible to enter. Remember that last year's Miss EBC went on to win the Miss Common Market contest and received a sports car and went on a world tour with visits to Brussels, Singapore and Hollywood!

First prize in this year's Miss EBC contest is an evening out with the compere of the contest, Pasha Mistel, and a holiday for the lucky winner and her mother in Acapulco, Mexico.

Second prize is a video cassette recorder and an evening out with your favourite EBC news reporter.

Dozens of other fantastic prizes for the runners-up.

Send a colour photograph of yourself with your full name, address and telephone number to EBC, EBC Centre, London.

# ROYAL BRITISH TOBACCO PROUDLY ANNOUNCE . . .

This summer in Hyde Park, London, the Royal Opera House, Covent Garden, will be giving a series of free, open-air evening performances every Saturday evening.

Top singers from all over the world will be performing in the operas, which include favourite works by Verdi, Puccini, Bizet and Donizetti. Already booked to appear are Placido Domenica, Luciano Pavaretto, Iliana Contrubesco and Renata Tabasco.

The performances begin on July 7th with 'Aida' and finish on August 25th with 'Madam Butterfly'.

A specially designed 50,000-seat arena will be built in the park for the opera season. There will be no advance booking for the performances. To get a seat, opera lovers will have to queue up on the day of the performance. Admission will be free, but to gain entry each person will need to have in his or her possession a packet from any brand of RBT cigarettes.

The complete series of performances are sponsored by Royal British Tobacco Ltd.

---

# acme management · dean street · london west one

### SNIFF'S WORLD TOUR ANNOUNCED

*The Sniffs, Britain's no. 1 rock group of the year, announce their first World Tour.*

*The first leg of their tour takes in venues in Amsterdam, Frankfurt, Vienna, Zurich, Paris and Madrid. From there the band fly on to Caracas, Rio de Janiero, Sao Paulo, Buenos Aires and Mexico City before starting their 10-city tour of the USA and Canada. From Vancouver, Canada, they fly across the Pacific to Tokyo, where they will play 5 nights in the largest stadium in the world - the mammoth 500,000-seat Shibuta Stadium. The final leg of the tour takes them to Australia for Christmas and back to England via Cairo and Rome. Their last concert of the tour will be in their home town of Ipswich.*

*This is the longest and most ambitious tour ever undertaken by a British band and in the course of the tour they will be seen and heard by more people than any other British band in the history of popular music.*

85

# MACTAVISH SHIPS AND ENGINEERING    GLASGOW

## £50M order for Scottish company

MacTavish Hovercraft Division announce that they have been successful in being given an order worth approximately £50 million for Type MT80 hovercraft. The order has been placed by the World Health Organization and the hovercraft are to be equipped as mobile health centres and hospitals. The order marks the start of WHO's new campaign to eradicate disease. It is estimated that 85% of the world's population lives within 40 km of water or land navigable by hovercraft.

The MT80 has been one of Britain's biggest export earners of the past few years. It has a cruising speed of 50 km/h and can travel over any reasonably flat surface including swamps and marshes. It can also cope with rough water with waves up to 5 metres in height.

Work has already started on the first of the 22 hovercraft ordered and the first 11 will be delivered within 12 months.

---

# ZONAPHONE UK – Pioneers in miniaturized audio

Zonaphone UK proudly announce that their revolutionary new ZONAPHONE 2000 will be on the market next month.
The ZONAPHONE 2000 is a miniature colour TV/stereo radio measuring only 15 cm x 10 cm x 10 cm.

It works on a totally new concept in rechargeable bronze batteries and costs virtually nothing to run.  The picture quality using the built-in aerial is superb, thanks to computer enhancement of the image using silicon chip technology, and the sound quality, using digital techniques, is of the highest quality. Stereo can be obtained by simply plugging the ZONAPHONE 2000 into a domestic hi-fi system.

The most remarkable feature of the ZONAPHONE 2000 is its price: only £99.99, with batteries included.  The ZONAPHONE 2000 is guaranteed for 2 years.

## EARTH TREMOR IN CALIFORNIA

There was an earth tremor to-day in San Francisco. At about 8
o'clock this morning just as the city was going to work, people
felt the ground move under their feet and watched buildings shake
and plant pots fall. The city's cable cars did a sort of dance
as they wobbled down the many hills. Fortunately nothing more
serious than a few cracks in the pink-washed buildings has
occurred, and the atmosphere here is far from panic. There is an
odd calm reigning over the city and people are speaking in hushed
voices of 'when it happens', referring of course to the
tremendous earthquake that is expected any time now. San
Francisco's last tremor was 2 years ago and last earthquake in
the early nineteen-hundreds.

## ROBBERY IN BOURNEMOUTH

£150,000 worth of jewellery and antiques has been stolen from the
home of the TV comedian Max Mygraves in Bournemouth. Mr
Mygraves, who began life as a docker in London's East End,
started his show business career in the radio show 'Bringing Up
Bertie', after which he became the star of the TV show 'Friday
Evening at the Pavilion'. His greatest success was in his own
show 'Max Jokes', after which he retired from show business.

He has made just one TV appearance each year in the
highly successful American show 'Max in Las Vegas'. He has been
living a quiet secluded life with his wife, Daphne, and his four
Labrador dogs in a suburb of Bournemouth popular with show
business people.

He said to the press today: 'I am not a millionaire and the
loss of all my jewellery and antiques is a very cruel blow. My
wife has been really upset by the stress it has caused her and
she has been on tranquillizers since it happened. Myself, I've
been drinking more than I should. Unless we get our possessions
back, we'll have to sell our house here and move back to London.'

## CAT SURVIVES JUMBO FLIGHT

Mr James Boot, who works as a luggage loader at Heathrow Airport, reported his cat, Tigger, missing on Saturday. Mr Boot's cat stays with him while he is working at the airport, because he would get very lonely left at home all day.

But 2 days after going missing, Tigger reappeared, very hungry and very cold. Mr Boot was unloading a 747 Jumbo jet from Toronto, when Tigger suddenly appeared from behind one of the cases in the hold.

Mr Boot told newsmen: 'I can only assume Tigger found his way onto the plane while my back was turned. He's never done anything like this before. He must have stowed away in the hold and stayed there all the way across the Atlantic and back again. He's lucky to be alive after his flight, but apart from needing a square meal, he seemed none the worse for wear.'

As the cat had obviously not left the plane in Canada, quarantine restrictions are not being applied. But Mr Boot's supervisor has put his foot down and banned Tigger from the airport. So now Tigger will have to stay at home by himself, even if he does get lonely.

## 747 HIJACKED BY GREEN LIBERATION MOVEMENT

An Eastern Airways Jumbo, on a flight from Singapore to Bangkok, was hijacked at 1.00 a.m. local time. There are 350 passengers on board. Details are unclear but it is thought that the hijackers are members of the Green Liberation movement.

A member of the airport ground staff remembers noticing that one of the passengers boarding the plane seemed particularly nervous, but she put it down to apprehension of boarding a Jumbo for the first time. Bangkok authorities have made no comment so far.

This is the third hijacking incident this week and people think that terrorists are copying each other.

The Green Liberation Movement claims to represent the peasants working on the tobacco plantations in the Third World and its aims are to raise their standard of living.

## ROUND THE WORLD BY BICYCLE

Jack Green, aged 59, has just returned from a tour of the world on a bicycle. He left his home in Streatham, South London, on June 4th 1979 and has just got home after pedalling round the globe.

He decided to make his trip after losing his job and he managed to earn enough to pay for his food and expenses during the trip by doing repairs to other people's bicycles. He nearly starved to death in India, lost his memory for a week in Japan, broke his leg in Canada and fell in love and got married in Mexico. His wife, also a keen cyclist, accompanied him on the last part of his trip.

## HAPPY EVENT AT CHESTER ZOO

Fu-Fu, the giant panda, to-day gave birth to twins at Chester Zoo. Mother and babies are doing well. This is the result of a successful mating last winter with the giant panda, Zapai, kept in Moscow Zoo.

Fu-Fu's keeper, Mr James Rowbotham, is delighted at the successful birth and says he will devote all his time, for the next two months, to caring for them. The babies will be kept with their mother as long as possible. If their mother rejects them, they will be hand-reared by Mr Rowbotham and his assistants. It is not known what quantity of dried milk a baby panda requires if bottle-fed, but Chester Zoo authorities are getting in a good supply.

The last attempted mating of giant pandas ended in failure when Chi-Chi was sent back from Moscow to London Zoo in disgrace.

## SNIFFS BANNED FROM USA

The Sniffs, whose record 'Hate you, Darling' has been No.1 in the charts for 2 months, have been declared prohibited immigrants by the Washington authorities. This means that they will be unable to do any of their proposed concerts in the USA.

The ban follows a statement by the group's drummer Ken Nostril, that 'The US government stinks'. It is also partly due to the obscene lyrics of their new LP 'Give America back to the Indians', which has shocked even some of the Sniffs' fans.

The EBC also announced a ban on the Sniffs: no Sniffs records will be played on EBC Radio ever again.

89

## DOG GETS AWARD

Mrs Janet Twigg's dog, Butch, spent the afternoon at Buckingham Palace today as the guest of the Queen. He was there to receive the Green Cross Gold Medal for Bravery for the rescue of a young child from drowning.

Last month, Butch, who lives in Felixstowe, saw Mary O'Hara get out of her depth in the sea and start crying for help. He jumped into the sea and swam out to Mary's rescue. She was able to grab his collar while he swam back to the beach. But for Butch's prompt action, little Mary would probably have drowned.

This afternoon, after being presented with his medal, Butch was introduced to the Royal corgis and was taken for a walk around the Royal gardens by Mrs Twigg. Commenting on her day at the Palace, Mrs Twigg said: 'It was really lovely. Her Majesty was ever so nice to us and we had a cup of tea with her. I felt really proud of my Butch'.

## NEW UNIFORM FOR POLICEWOMEN

Metropolitan Police announced a new uniform for policewomen in the London area. It marks a departure from the traditional navy jacket and skirt worn since the inception of the Women's Police Force in 1920. The new uniform will be far more femimine – with a flared, calf-length skirt, white blouse with frilled collar and cuffs and a fitted single-breasted jacket. Colour will depend on the area the policewomen usually work in: it will be red in the City of Westminster, bottle green in Central London and royal blue in the Greater London area.

A spokeswoman for the policewomen said they were delighted with the change because it was high time policewomen had a new image.

## PLANE CRASH IN YUGOSLAVIA

An Olympic Airways Boeing 727 carrying 120 passengers crashed into the Dinaric mountains near Split at 4.00 a.m. local time. All passengers and crew are feared dead. The plane was on its way from Dubrovnik to Venice. There were hazardous weather conditions when the plane left Dubrovnik and the last radio communication was when the pilot reported losing power in three engines.

## MORE FIGHTING BETWEEN FORCES OF ZAMFAZI AND SIRAZO

A fresh outbreak of fighting has taken place along the disputed border of Zamfazi and Sirazo.  Troops from both countries clashed along a two-mile stretch of the Canga river.  Leaders in both countries are refusing to meet to discuss the crisis and advisers from both USSR and USA are reported to have been seen in the capital of Zamfazi, Bofuza.

Casualties have been few but a British mercenary leader in Sirazo feared that, with weapons flowing in to both sides from other countries, the fighting would take a more grisly turn. British mercenaries are estimated at 500.

The dispute began three months ago when Sirazo gained full independence from Britain and failed to reach agreement with Zamfazi about territorial limitation.  Sirazo is one of the world's leading producers of zinc.

## POSTMAN BITES DOG

Geoff Smith of Winton loves dogs, but when he's delivering letters, he finds not all dogs love him.  One particular dog called Spot, who lives at No.1 Strouden Road, was one of Geoff's biggest enemies.  Whenever Geoff approached his owner's house, Spot used to lie in wait and jump out on Geoff, barking and snapping at his ankles.

Then, one day, Geoff slipped on a patch of ice and went sprawling on the garden path of No.1 Strouden Road.  Spot saw this as his big chance: he jumped onto Geoff's back and tried to bite his neck.  Quick as a flash Geoff, whose hands were full of letters, bit Spot on the leg.

Mr Smith said later: 'It was the only thing I could do.  I don't approve of cruelty to animals, but that dog really had it coming.  Anyway, since that day I've had no trouble at No.1.  Spot always hides round the back of the house when he hears me coming.'

## SNIFFS BANNED AGAIN

Following the ban by the USA on the Sniffs, 5 other countries on their tour itinerary have banned them from appearing.  A spokesman for the Australian government said: 'We have no objection to the political attitudes of the group.  What we do object to is their bad language, dirty clothes and uncivilized behaviour.  They also claim that they never wash.  This sort of thing can only have a bad influence on the young people of my country.'

Not only Australia but also Brazil, Argentina, France and Italy have banned the Sniffs from appearing.

## HEART TRANSPLANT SUCCESSFUL

The heart transplant carried out by Mr Cornelius Brown at
Papworth Hospital near Cambridge seems to have been successful.
Mr Brown carried out the operation on Charles Hoffman of Penzance
in Cornwall.

Mr Hoffman, aged 53, worked as a lathe operator in a factory
and has been in poor health since a heart attack last year.
After Mr Cornelius Brown's previous successes at Papworth
Hospital, Mr Hoffman's work-mates decided to club together to pay
for their old friend's operation. They held raffles, organized
dances and jumble sales and advertized on local radio and
television for donations. In 3 months they managed to raise the
£8000 needed to pay for the operation.

Mr Hoffman answered questions from the press yesterday: 'My
doctor told me I had 6 months to live. I don't know how I can
thank my pals in the factory. Now I feel on top of the world –
in fact, I feel as right as rain.'

## TEACHERS TO STRIKE

Members of the National Teachers Union are to go on strike from
Monday next. Talks between their leaders and the Government
broke down this morning after three days of negotiation. The
teachers are demanding a 30 per cent pay increase and claim that,
in relation to the rest of the working population, they are
grossly underpaid. The Government say that any pay increase for
teachers would be very inflationary and lead to claims from all
other public employees. Teachers claim that they are a special
case and that this pay rise would not be inflationary.

The strike will close all state schools and pupils will be
sent home. The Teachers Union say that their strike will
continue indefinitely until their demands are met.

O-level and A-level examinations, which were to be held
during the next two weeks, are likely to be cancelled  unless
volunteer teachers can be persuaded to invigilate pupils taking
these exams.

## TV AND RADIO STRIKE CALLED OFF

Union leaders have called off their threatened strike after talks
with the employers. Programmes this evening will be broadcast as
normal.

92

## SEXTUPLETS BORN IN NEW ZEALAND

A Palmerston North woman was safely delivered of sextuplets at
Palmerston General Hospital this morning. Mrs Felicity James,
aged 25, gave birth to two girls and four boys, the babies each
weigh approximately 1 kilogram and are being kept in incubators.
They are all healthy.

Mrs James originally comes from Bolton in Lancashire, where
she used to work at Craig's Textile Mills.

This is the second live birth of sextuplets in recent
months. The last was in Toronto in June when Mrs Phillipa Tring
had six girls.

Both women were taking a fertility pill. There have been
many cases of unsuccessful multiple births throughout the western
world in recent years.

## JEWELLERY AND ANTIQUES RETURNED

This afternoon at 3 o'clock, there was a knock at the door of TV
star Max Mygraves' home in Bournemouth and his stolen property
was handed back to him.

Mr Mygraves described the event to newsmen: 'Shortly before
tea, there was a knock at the door and a man with a mask over his
face handed me a large sack containing all my stolen property.
He said he was sorry he had stolen it. He said that he hadn't
realized that it was my house he had robbed. He told me I was
one of his favourite stars and that he was so ashamed of what he
had done that he wanted to give himself up to the police. I told
him not to do that but to promise never to steal anything ever
again. He gave me his word and I have told the police that the
case should now be dropped.'

## KIDNAPPING IN BRAZIL

The 21-year-old son of the coffee millionaire, Philip Mendes de
Felipe, was kidnapped outside the University in Sao Paulo to-day.
Sergio Mendes de Felipe came out of his class at lunch-time with
other students and was hustled into a car by four men
masquerading as students. The men were reported to have been
carrying guns. So far no news has come of their demands. The
Mendes family has coffee plantations and processing plants worth
undisclosed millions and Mr Mendes de Felipe is one of the most
powerful men in Brazil providing, as he does, an enormous
contribution to the export trade. Mr Felipe's eldest daughter,
Hilda, married a junior army officer earlier this year.

## £500,000 POOLS WIN

Mr and Mrs Walter Brown of Coventry won £495,281.55 on this
week's football pools. They were presented with their cheque at
the Dorchester Hotel in London's Park Lane by Freddy Roberts,
star of the TV show 'Not now mum, it's too hot'.

After being toasted in brown ale, Mr Brown's favourite
drink, the couple were interviewed by the press. Said Mrs Brown:
'We're really over the moon about our good luck. We chose the
matches with a pin and we nearly forgot to send off the coupon.
The first thing we're going to do is to buy a new bungalow.
We've lived all our married life in a council flat and we've
always dreamed of having a bungalow. Apart from that we're not
going to go on a spending spree just yet. We want to sit down
and think about it first.'

## CURE FOR CANCER ANNOUNCED

The World Health Organisation has just announced a spectacular
advance in the fight against cancer. Millions of dollars have
been spent on research into this disease, one of the most wide-
spread and deadly in the industrialised countries. The research
team has isolated an organism which promotes growth of cancerous
cells and have discovered an antidote to its development. They
have performed thousands of successful experiments in animals
suffering from various forms of cancer and in 95% of the cases,
the antidote has halted the cancerous growth completely. The
research team has been very careful to announce their results
only after prolonged experimentation and they are not claiming
that this is a 100% successful cure for human suffering from
cancer. However, the tests they have carried out on volunteer
human guinea-pigs have been successful, according to the team.

## BRAZILIAN KIDNAPPING - LATEST

Sergio Mendes de Felipe's kidnappers have demanded a million
dollar ransom and a guarantee of improved working conditions for
people in the de Felipe's coffee processing factories.

## FRENCH KIDNAPPING - LATEST

In spite of objections from the police, M Rabelais has agreed to
pay the ransom the kidnappers are demanding.

SNIFFS' WORLD TOUR CANCELLED

After the cancellation of more of their concerts on their world tour, the Sniffs have called off the tour.

Their manager, Peter Bridge, said today: 'The world isn't ready for the Sniffs yet. Musically and politically, they're 10 years ahead of their time. Still it's the world's loss, not ours. The tour wasn't going to make any money anyway.'

The only concert that will still take place is the last one, planned for their home town, Ipswich. The group say that it's their local and most loyal fans they most want to play for.

A further comment from the Sniffs' lead singer, Johhny X. Hale: 'It's typical of the middle-class, middle-aged establishment in every country that they won't let their children hear what we have to say. Let me tell them all right now that one day the whole world will listen to what we have to say.'

# The Arts Centre

## Description

The participants are divided into groups, representing different members of the management and staff of the Arts Centre. Each group begins by planning the programme of events at the Centre for the next six months, paying particular attention to its own specialist area.

What the participants do *not* know in advance, is that they are going to have to cope with rumours and letters concerning a serious financial crisis. The Board of Directors, via the department managers, are going to have to impose economy cuts, declare redundancies among the staff and perhaps close down some departments. The Arts Centre is a 'model' of a hierarchical organization, where the staff only have personal contact with their immediate superiors or juniors. The 'Rules of the Simulation' allow for only one representative of the staff of each department (the 'Union Representative') to have access to the Board.

First of all, each group is issued with their day's work, which is to begin planning the future programme of the Centre. Then, one by one, each group hears different rumours on the cassette and is given different letters. Each group discusses the changing situation and decides what action to take.

The simulation has no predictable ending. What happens in the end depends on what the participants decide to do and their reaction to what other groups decide to do. In this respect it is very different from the earlier simulations in this book. Not even the Controller knows quite what will happen. This makes it a very exciting simulation but not one to be tackled before some of the more straightforward ones have been done.

(Do not reveal *any* of this information to the participants.)

## Assigning roles and arranging groups

If you know your participants very well, you may be able to assign their roles in accordance with their interests: real-life businessmen could be the Directors, real theatre fans could be the Producer and the Actors and real cinema buffs could be the Cinema staff and so on. But probably you will need to form well-balanced groups on the basis of mixed abilities, nationalities, personalities and sexes.

With 28 to 30 participants, roles should be assigned as follows:

*Group A*    BOARD OF DIRECTORS
Four directors with special responsibilities: Thomas (theatre), Masters (music), Richards (restaurant), Cecil (cinema) and an optional Chairman of the Board – Dixon.

*Group B*    MANAGEMENT
Taylor (theatre manager), Mortimer (concert hall manager), Rose (restaurant manager), Carter (cinema manager) and an optional deputy manager who stands in for any manager who is on holiday – Driver.

*Group C*    THEATRE
Theobald, Thorogood, Thorpe, Thurlow and Thornton (producer and actors).

*Group D*    CONCERT HALL
Morris, Metcalfe, Murray, Mitchell and Matthews (musicians).

*Group E*    RESTAURANT
Robertson, Ross, Riggs, Reynolds and Rogers (staff members).

*Group F*    CINEMA
Clarke, Cooper, Crocker, Cox and Corbett (staff members).

This chart will help you to distribute and assign roles with different class sizes:

| Number of participants | 10 | 12 | 15 | 19 | 24 |
|---|---|---|---|---|---|
| Directors: | 2 | 3 | 3 | 3 | 4 |
| Managers: | 2 | 3 | 3 | 4 | 4 |
| Staff: | 6 | 6 | 9 | 12 | 16 |
| | in 3 | in 3 | in 4 | in 4 | in 4 |
| | Depts | Depts | Depts | Depts | Depts |

(leave out the least interesting roles)

## Organizing time and arranging space

*Preparation*    The talking points, useful language and practice activities take about 45 minutes – longer if your students find a lot of unfamiliar words in the vocabulary lists.

The Arts Centre

*The simulation*    For the simulation itself, you'll need an uninterrupted period of 1½ – 4 hours. There should be no breaks in case there is unofficial contact between participants from different groups.

In this specimen timetable the whole simulation is fitted into 3 hours (9.00-12.00) or 1½ hours (19.00-20.30):

| | | |
|---|---|---|
| 9.00 | Give out role information and send everyone to their respective areas. Allow time for reading and questions. | 19.00 |
| 9.15 | Groups start making their plans for the Arts Centre according to their role information sheet. | 19.10 |
| 9.40 | Directors receive letter from County Council. Staff and Management hear Rumour 1 on cassette. | 19.25 |
| 9.50 | Directors tell Management about their proposed cuts – they may need prompting to do this.<br>Staff hear Rumour 2 on cassette. | 19.35 |
| 10.00 | Each manager tells his or her staff about the cuts.<br>Directors receive letter from Lord Glass. | 19.45 |
| 10.30 | Staff hear Rumour 3 and then Management hear Rumour 4 and then the Board hear Rumour 5. | 19.55 |
| 10.40 | Each staff department receives a letter from its Union Headquarters. | 20.05 |
| 11.30 | Controller decides whether a General Meeting should be held now or to let the simulation continue. | 20.15 |
| 12.00 | End of simulation. It can just stop abruptly without any neat dénouement. | 20.30 |

The times given are approximate because the 'action' of this simulation depends heavily on what the participants decide to do at various stages of the game.

Each group needs its own separate area. Ideally, the Board should have its own room, the Management its own room and the staff their own areas of a third room. Alternatively, the Board and Management could share a room, but they *must* be in separate areas. With a small number of participants, different areas of the same room are suitable for everyone, but again the areas must be separated to prevent the participants from breaking the rules and communicating with people they shouldn't.

*Follow-up*    The follow-up discussion can take place the same day as the simulation after a break, or when the class next meets. The discussion takes 30 to 45 minutes.

## What you need

Two to five photocopies of each of the role information sheets on pages 104 to 109. Each participant's name and role should be filled in like this:

> You are ..... *Maria Thomas* .....
>
> You are a member of the Board of Directors, with special
>
> responsibility for ..... *the Theatre* .....

or

> You are ..... *Jean-Pierre Reynolds* .....
>
> You work in the Restaurant at the Arts Centre.

One photocopy of each of the letters on pages 110 to 115.
A badge or label for each participant.
The cassette with the five rumours on and one cassette player.
Your own list of participants and their roles and a schedule of events.

## Preparation

*Talking points*
1 Spend a few minutes on the talking points. Perhaps get the students to start off in groups.

*Useful language*
2 Check that everyone understands everything and that they can pronounce everything correctly.

*Practice activities*
3 Students working in groups should add more words to the vocabulary lists. Go round helping as requested. Get everyone to pool their suggestions when they are ready.

4 Working in pairs, the students should test each other on the vocabulary. A very advanced class may not need to do this activity if they know all the words already.

*Before the simulation begins*
5 Make sure that everyone looks carefully at the information on pages 42 to 45 of the Participant's Book. If necessary, run through any points you think may be tricky.

## The simulation

1 Make sure everyone knows the rules of the simulation on page 41 of the Participant's Book. Look at them again together just in case, perhaps.

---

### Rules of the simulation

1 You are only allowed to speak to the staff immediately above you or immediately below you in the hierarchy of the organization. But you are allowed to communicate in writing with anyone.

2 The only exception to Rule 1 is that Union Representatives can arrange a meeting with the individual Director responsible for their department, but only on a one-to-one basis.

3 The Controller must be informed before a meeting of any kind takes place.

4 The Controller must be informed of the outcome of any meeting, even if no important decisions have been made.

---

2 Give everyone their role information sheet (photocopied from pages 104 to 109) with their name and role filled in.

3 Send the participants to their respective rooms or areas without allowing them to talk to any other participants. Allow enough time for reading and questions before you declare the simulation open.

4 Each group follows the instructions on its role information sheet and starts work on its plans. Allow them 20 to 30 minutes to do this.

5 Give the 'Letter from the County Council' (photocopied from page 110) to the Board of Directors and play Rumour 1 on the cassette to the Management and the Staff in the departments.

**Rumour 1**

A: ...Hallo, Bill, I've just heard something rather worrying.
B: Oh, yeah, what's that?
A: Someone told me that they aren't going to raise our salaries next month.
B: But they've got to – it's in our contract. We're due for our quarterly cost of living adjustment.
A: Well, I know that, but apparently the Centre's been making a

loss and they haven't got the money to pay us the extra.

B: I don't really believe it. You've probably got hold of the wrong end of the stick or something. They just can't do that.

A: Perhaps you're right, anyway....

(If the Board are sharing the same room as the Management, it might be best to play Rumour 1 to the Management in the corridor or in the room where the Staff are.)

6 Soon after this, the Directors will tell the Management about the proposed cuts – if they don't, they may need some prompting to do so. When this is happening, play Rumour 2 to the Staff:

**Rumour 2**

C: ... by the way, Don, have you heard anyone talking about redundancies lately?

D: What, here at the Arts Centre?

C: Yes, here. You see, I heard two of the cleaners talking about it.

D: One of the things you learn very quickly is that it's the cleaners who find out about things first in a place like this.

C: That's right and they were saying that the Directors are going to make half the permanent staff redundant.

D: That's ridiculous. They couldn't run the place without this many staff. We're overworked as it is, aren't we?

C: Yes, but they could close down one or two departments, couldn't they?

D: You mean the restaurant? They wouldn't do that, would they?

C: It might not be the restaurant, it might be the...

(If the Staff are sharing the same room as the Management or Board, it's best to take one member of each department outside the room to hear Rumour 2 and then report back to their colleagues what they've overheard.)

7 Soon after this, each Manager will tell his or her own staff about the cuts. When this is happening, give the Directors the 'Letter from Lord Class' (photocopied from page 111).

8 By this time, the simulation may well have developed its own momentum. If so, there is no point in intervening unless the rules of the simulation are being disobeyed. For example, the Controller *must* be informed beforehand of any meetings and afterwards of their outcome.

9 At about the half-way point, play the remaining rumours to the relevant groups. First Rumour 3 to the Staff only:

**Rumour 3**

E: ...I'm not one to spread rumours, but...

F: Yes?

E: Well, don't tell anyone *I* told you, but a little bird told me that none of us are going to get paid this month.

F: Not get paid?!

E: Not according to my source, anyway. It seems they're in dire financial trouble and they haven't got enough money in the bank to cover our salaries.

101

*F:* What? That's terrible. Who told you all this?
*E:* Ah, that's something I can't tell you. All I can say is...

(To prevent the Management or Board from overhearing in a shared room, it may be best to let some of the Staff hear Rumour 3 outside the room.)

10 Next, play Rumour 4 to the Management only:

**Rumour 4**

*G:* Harry, I've just heard something rather interesting.
*H:* Oh yes?
*G:* Hmm. You've heard this talk about cutting down on the number of staff in each department?
*H:* Of course, everyone's talking about it.
*G:* Well, apparently, they're going to reduce the number of managers too.
*H:* You must have misunderstood what someone was saying.
*G:* I don't think so. You know as well as I do that this place is top-heavy. It'd be no loss to us if they sacked the entire management and let the Board take over the running of the Centre.
*H:* Come on, George, that's going a bit far.
*G:* Just you wait and see. Mark my words, in a month or so I bet at least two of our managers'll be looking for new jobs...

(To prevent the Board from overhearing in a shared room, let the Management hear Rumour 4 outside the room.)

11 Next, play Rumour 5 to the Board of Directors only:

**Rumour 5**

*I:* Finished doing upstairs yet, Jane?
*J:* I've done the walls, but I've still got the hoovering to do.
*I:* Feel like a smoke?
*J:* Don't mind if I do, thanks.
*I:* Do you think they will go on strike?
*J:* Well, they've been saying they will, but it's hard to say if they really mean it.
*I:* Reason I ask is that I heard two of those union blokes talking about 'industrial action' and you know what that means, don't you?
*J:* But they're not like that here, are they? I mean, you couldn't call them militants, now could you?
*I:* Well, they didn't use to be but times have changed and now they...

(To prevent anyone else overhearing in a shared room, let the Board hear this outside the room.)

12 Soon after this give each Staff department its 'Letter from Union Headquarters' (photocopied from pages 112 to 115).

13 If by this time a stalemate has developed, you could, for example, encourage further meetings between the Union Representatives and the Directors, or the Management could be encouraged to talk to their Staff again. Or you could invent further rumours and write them on slips of paper and give them to selected participants. Or you could compose another letter or two.

By and large, though, the Controller should allow the participants to do what they think fit, even if it's quite obvious to you that they will regret the consequences.

But if by this time the situation is becoming too volatile, it might just be advisable for you to step in and restore order by, for example, sending the over-aggressive group back to its original area to write a 'Statement to the Press' about their views.

14 A full meeting to 'thrash things out' could be arranged by the Controller to round things off, starting about half an hour before the end.

Or you may prefer to end it abruptly at this point and have the follow-up discussion after a short break. This will mean that everyone can speculate what might have happened if there had been more time and what the eventual outcome would have been.

Or, if things are going well, allow the simulation to continue until your time is up. Then the follow-up discussion can be held after the written work has been done.

15 Set the written work.

## Follow-up

1 The follow-up discussion for this simulation can be done after a short break when the simulation itself has finished. Leave this option open in case you decide to cut the simulation short for any reason. Normally, however, it would be done later so that the participants have more time to consider their answers to the questions.

2 See what everyone thinks in answer to the questions. Make your own comments on their communicative performance.

3 If the simulation ended inconclusively, what does everyone think would have happened in the end? What were they each about to do when the simulation ended?

4 Their plans for the next six months at the Arts Centre were probably pushed aside by more pressing events in the simulation. Let each group describe its plans if there's time.

5 Set the written work if you haven't already set it.

You are .....................................................

You are a member of the Board of Directors, with special

responsibility for .....................................................

The Arts Centre is in severe financial trouble. There is only one way to solve the problem:

**Make drastic economy cuts to save money.**

If you can cut the Centre's expenditure, the County Council might agree to increase the amount of its subsidy to the Centre. Here are some of the reasons for the present crisis:

CONCERT HALL: Too many loss-making concerts.
Expensive orchestra to pay and keep busy.

THEATRE: Too many unprofitable performances by guest companies.
New Arts Centre company of actors overstaffed.
Local audiences dislike 'experimental' and 'classical' drama.

RESTAURANT: Not enough customers.
Local people don't like fancy foreign food, they want good honest traditional British food.
A cafeteria would be much cheaper to run than a restaurant with full table service.

CINEMA: Some days the cinema is half-empty.
There are plenty of successful commercial cinemas in the area.

Here are some of the economy measures you could take:

1 Raise ticket prices (now £1 cinema, £2 theatre and concert hall).
2 Raise programme prices (now 30p for 10-page programme).
3 Save on heating (now constant 20°C).
4 Save on lighting (remove every other light bulb in staff-only areas).
5 Freeze staff salaries (they would be getting an inflation-adjusted increase next month).
6 Reduce numbers of staff in each department.
7 Close down most unprofitable departments and make staff redundant.

Decide on the measures you are going to take and then tell your manager to tell his staff at a departmental meeting.

You are ......................................................

You are the manager of the ......................................................

1  You have asked your staff to consider the next 6 months and to suggest ways in which the service offered by your department could be improved. They are now working on their suggestions for the next 6 months' programme.

2  Meanwhile, you and the other managers have to work out your solutions to this major problem:

**The Arts Centre doesn't attract enough people.**

Here is an outline of some of the problems in detail:

| | |
|---|---|
| CONCERT HALL: | The hall is nearly empty when there are symphony concerts or chamber concerts on. The only concerts which sell out are the Country and Western Evening and middle-of-the-road family shows. |
| THEATRE: | Only filled when local amateur groups are doing shows (relations and friends of the cast) or for Christmas pantomime or for good professional whodunit. Modern drama particularly unpopular. |
| RESTAURANT: | The 'Speciality Months' experiment has not been a success. Business Lunches make a profit, but otherwise the restaurant is half empty every evening except Saturday. |
| CINEMA: | Other local cinemas do good business. Local people say the programme is too 'arty'. |
| CHILDREN: | How can more children be persuaded to attend the Centre? Once they attend regularly they'll go on attending. |
| PUBLICITY: | How can this be improved? |

Prepare your ideas on attracting more people to the Centre. Remember, by the way, that it is your responsibility to 'stimulate the cultural life of the county' as well as to pull in as many customers as possible.

Submit your recommendations to the Board of Directors and explain them to the staff of your department when you are ready.

You are ........................................................

You work in the Concert Hall at the Arts Centre.

1 Elect a Union Representative (Shop Steward).
2 Your manager has asked you to prepare your recommendations for the future programme of your department. Work out a balanced and interesting programme of concerts for the next 6 months. Remember that it is your responsibility to 'stimulate the cultural life of the county' as well as to attract a wide audience to the Concert Hall.

Here are some points you might want to consider:—

| | |
|---|---|
| ORCHESTRAL MUSIC: | Popular classics or more demanding works? What works can you suggest for the programme? |
| CHAMBER MUSIC: | String quartets? Piano recitals? These attract small audiences but very high quality of performance. |
| BIG NAME ROCK BANDS: | Very popular, not very profitable. Suggestions for groups to book? |
| MIDDLE-OF-THE-ROAD MUSIC: | Very popular and profitable but of poor quality. Suggestions of bands or singers? |
| LOCAL POP GROUPS: | Showcase for local talent, very cheap, reasonably popular. |
| FOLK MUSIC: | Small but enthusiastic audiences. Local singers (free) or famous names (expensive)? |
| JAZZ: | Local bands or star guests? A lot of jazz played locally in clubs and pubs. |
| REGULAR EVENTS: | Under 16's Disco, Ballroom Dancing, Country and Western Evening — all very popular but should they be part of an *Arts* Centre programme? |
| CHILDREN: | How can more children be attracted to the Centre? |

Prepare your recommendations, including details of suggested works and musicians, for the Concert Hall Manager to see.

*The Arts Centre*

You are .....................................................

You work in the Restaurant at the Arts Centre.

1  Elect a Union Representative (Shop Steward).
2  Your manager has asked you to prepare your recommendations for the restaurant for the next 6 months. Work out a balanced and appetizing set of menus.
   Remember that there are plenty of other restaurants in the area, so try to make your restaurant really *different*!

Here are some points you might want to consider:—

INTERNATIONAL DISHES: Should you offer 'Speciality Months', as you have been doing?
What countries should be represented?
What particular dishes do you suggest?

BRITISH FOOD: A traditional Sunday lunch?
Old-fashioned English food?

COFFEE SHOP: What snacks and light refreshments?
Can you suggest any unusual cakes or savouries?

BAR: How can more people be attracted to the bar?
How can it be different from the normal run of pubs?
Entertainment?
Link-up with theatre/concert hall perform-ances?

CHILDREN: How can more children be attracted to eat in the Centre?
Special children's menus? What?

Prepare your recommendations, including details of menus and suggested improvements, for the Restaurant Manager to see.

*The Arts Centre*

You are ....................................................

You work in the Theatre at the Arts Centre.

1  Elect a Union Representative (Shop Steward).
2  Your manager has asked you to prepare your recommendations for
   the future programme of the Theatre. Work out a balanced and
   interesting programme, involving performances by other companies
   of actors as well as by your own company. Remember that it is your
   responsibility to 'stimulate the cultural life of the county' as well as to
   pull in large audiences.

   Here are some of the points you might want to consider:–

SHAKESPEARE:               School exams: plays on the syllabus will
                           bring in big parties.
                           A theatre must perform the classics, not
                           just popular modern plays.
                           If Shakespeare, which plays?
MODERN ENGLISH DRAMA:      High quality, experimental plays – not
                           very popular with locals.
INTERNATIONAL DRAMA:       Plays by foreign dramatists?
                           Suggestions of suitable plays?
POPULAR PLAYS:             Light comedy and whodunits –
                           poor quality but very good audiences.
MUSICALS AND SHOWS:        Small budget means these can't be up to
                           West End standards.
                           Is it worth trying to perform shows like
                           these in such a small theatre?
                           Very popular but unprofitable.
OPERA:                     Performances by touring companies?
                           Theatre half-empty but high quality
                           performances.
AMATEUR SHOWS:             Big local audience for these (relations
                           and friends of the cast?), but standard
                           poor.
CHILDREN:                  How can we attract more children to the
                           Theatre?

Prepare your recommendations, including details of suggested plays and
improvements, for the Theatre Manager to see.

You are ..................................................

You work in the Cinema at the Arts Centre.

1 Elect a Union Representative (Shop Steward).
2 Your manager has asked you to prepare your recommendations for the future programme of the Cinema. Consider the programme for the next 6 months and suggest what films should be booked. Remember that there are other cinemas in the area, so what you show in your cinema must be really *special*!

Here are some points you might want to consider:–

| | |
|---|---|
| PROGRAMME CHANGE: | Different films every day or every week? Double bills or single films? |
| NEW RELEASES: | New films will make money but this would put the Centre in direct competition with commercial cinemas. Family shows or adult films? |
| CLASSICS: | The history of the cinema illustrated? Shown on TV, but not the same as on the big screen. |
| 'ART FILMS': | Critically acclaimed but not widely distributed films – a taste of London in our area? May be unpopular – not released because of potentially small audience? |
| SEASONS OF FILMS: | Great directors? Themes: westerns, science fiction, historical, crime, romantic? |
| FOREIGN FILMS: | What countries? Any specific suggestions of films? Subtitles or dubbed into English? |
| CHILDREN: | Can we do better than showing Walt Disney films to attract more children and get them into the habit of coming to our cinema? |

Prepare your recommendations, including details of particular films and types of programme, for the Cinema Manager to see.

# COUNTY HALL, BARCHESTER, BARSETSHIRE

```
The Chairman
Board of Directors                    Your ref
The Arts Centre
Framley                               Our ref
Barsetshire
```

Dear Mr Dixon,

   It has come to our attention that the Arts Centre is in severe financial difficulties. We wish to make it clear that there is no prospect whatsoever of the County Council grant being increased this year to cover the losses your Centre has been making. In fact, in these hard times of recession and inflation, we should like to give you notice of the fact that the subsidy will not even be increased to cover the increase in the cost of living.

   We can only suppose that the losses you have been making are due to poor financial management by the board. It is essential that you impose severe economic measures to reduce your expenditure and make the Arts Centre as cost-effective as possible. If you do not do this, you will be running the risk of losing the County Council grant altogether.

             Yours faithfully,
             for the County Council,


             M. Lloyd

             M. Lloyd, County Treasurer

# the class organization FIFTY PARK LANE LONDON

The Chairman
Board of Directors
The Arts Centre
Framley
Barsetshire

Dear Sir,

May I take this opportunity of writing to you in confidence to put forward a proposition which may be to our mutual advantage. My organization would be prepared to take over the running of the Arts Centre with a view to turning it into a viable commercial enterprise. As you are no doubt aware, we have a great deal of experience in the running of leisure centres, cinemas and theatres throughout the country.

I fully realize that we shall have to come to a mutually agreeable financial arrangement, but I can assure you most sincerely that I will offer a more than generous price, based on the current market value of the premises. We would keep the concert hall, theatre and cinema open, but the restaurant is not well-sited or well-equipped and we would propose closing it.

There would be one condition upon which I must insist, and that is that your staff would be replaced by Class Organization Staff.

I look forward to hearing your reaction to my proposal.

Yours most sincerely,

*Arthur J. Class*

Arthur J. Class

*The Arts Centre*

## MUSICIANS' UNION HEADQUARTERS
14 Wardour Street
London W1

Chief Shop Steward

Concert Hall

The Arts Centre

Framley

Barsetshire


Dear Brother/Sister,

     It has come to our notice that there has been talk in your unit of taking unofficial industrial action against your Management and Board of Directors. Although I sympathize with your point of view vis-à-vis the stubborn intransigence of your Management, I cannot lend official support to any threat of a strike.

     It is irresponsible of your members to use such a threat when the channels of communication are still open and negotiation is still possible.

     Let me make our Union Headquarters' viewpoint quite clear: you must continue to talk and not go on strike. An unofficial strike would not gain the support of the Union.

               Yours fraternally,

               G. Harris

# Actors' Union Headquarters
### Twelve Shaftesbury Avenue
### London W1

Chief Shop Steward,
The Arts Centre Theatre,
Framley,
Barsetshire


Dear Brother/Sister,

It has come to our notice that there has been
talk in your unit of taking unofficial industrial
action against your Management and Board of
Directors. Although I sympathize with your point of
view vis-à-vis the stubborn intransigence of your
Management, I cannot lend official support to the
threat of a strike.

It is irresponsible of your members to use such
a threat when the channels of communication are
still open and negotiation is still possible.

Let me make our Union Headquarters' viewpoint
quite clear: you must continue to talk and not go on
strike. An unofficial strike would not gain the
support of the Union.


                    Yours fraternally,

                    Richard Wilson

## Catering and Allied Trades Association (CATA)
NATIONAL HEADQUARTERS, 77 Piccadilly, London W1

```
Chief Shop Steward
The Arts Centre (Catering Department)
Framley
Barsetshire
```

Dear Brother/Sister,

It has come to our notice that there has been talk in your unit of taking unofficial industrial action against your Management and Board of Directors. Although I sympathize with your point of view vis-à-vis the stubborn intransigence of your Management, I cannot lend official support to a strike threat.

It is irresponsible of your members to use such a threat when the channels of communication are still open and negotiation is still possible.

Let me make our Union Headquarters' viewpoint quite clear: you must continue to talk and not go on strike. An unofficial strike would not gain the support of the Union.

Yours fraternally,

*D.C. Jackson*

*The Arts Centre*

# SOCIETY OF PROJECTIONISTS AND CINEMA EMPLOYEES HEADQUARTERS
## 99 Leicester Square London W1

Chief Shop Steward
The Arts Centre Cinema
Framley
Barsetshire


Dear Brother/Sister,

It has come to our notice that there has been talk in your unit of taking unofficial industrial action against your Management and Board of Directors. Although I sympathize with your point of view vis-à-vis the stubborn intransigence of your Management, I cannot lend official support to the threat of a strike.

It is irresponsible of your members to use such a threat when the channels of communication are still open and negotiation is still possible.

Let me make our Union Headquarters' viewpoint quite clear: you must continue to talk and not go on strike. An unofficial strike would not gain the support of the Union.

Yours fraternally,

*C. R. Newman*

# Our Show

## Description

This simulation is very straightforward, but for its success it depends on participants who have had experience of working together in teams. The participants also need to be capable of preparing work at home before the simulation begins, to provide some of the content of their programme.

Each team needs a cassette recorder and the items for the programme are recorded one by one during the simulation, instead of being recorded all together at the end. However, if you are using video with several teams or if you only have one room for several teams to work in, there will have to be staggered deadlines so that each team finishes at a different time.

Note that the participants have to be divided into teams several days *before* the simulation, so that they can do the necessary advance preparation. If the participants agree, students from other classes could be invited to the playback session. It may inspire them to similar work!

The show that each team produces should reflect the interests and ideas of the members of the team, which makes *Our Show* a much more personal event than the other simulations. The participants may still decide to role-play some of the time, but the decision is theirs – in other words, it's *their* show!

## Arranging groups

If you have thirty participants there could be three or four teams of seven to ten participants. With only ten participants, two teams of five are better than one team of ten. As far as possible, the teams should consist of students who know each other well and have worked together before. On the other hand, each team should contain people with different interests and from different backgrounds.

The most important thing is to arrange the groups several days before the simulation.

## Organizing time and arranging space

*Preparation*   The only language preparation needed is a quick revision of some of the phrases and expressions practised in the earlier broadcast simulations. The teams should get together several days before the simulation to discuss what they're going to do. After discussing the talking points for a few minutes, allow the teams 10 to 15 minutes of class time to meet and exchange ideas.

*The simulation*   Ideally an uninterrupted period of 2 to 3 hours is needed. 1½ hours is long enough, provided that plenty of advance preparation has been done by the participants.

You will need to decide in advance how long each programme is going to be. Three or four teams producing 10-minute programmes or two teams producing 15-minute programmes are suggested.

With each team using its own cassette recorder and aiming to finish at the same time, there are no timetable problems. However, if the programmes are to be recorded in a central 'studio' or on video, staggered deadlines will be necessary. Allow each team an extra 5 to 10 minutes between each recording to absorb delays.

It is best if each team has its own room to work and make its recording in. Separate areas of the same room are adequate, but it's still worth finding a spare room elsewhere for the teams to go to for their recordings. Alternatively, have staggered deadlines.

The recording should be played back as soon as possible afterwards, so allow time for this in your schedule.

Here is a specimen timetable, fitting the whole simulation and playback of recordings into 3 hours, with three teams producing 10-minute shows:

9.00  Teams go to their rooms and start work discussing, preparing and recording their programmes.
11.20  Deadline for all the recordings to be ready.
Short break.
11.30  The three recordings are played back.
12.00  Set written work. Finish.

*Follow-up*   The discussion lasts 15 to 30 minutes.

## What you need

(No photocopying is needed for this simulation.)

A cassette recorder and a blank cassette for each team.
Some copies of recent local newspapers (if available).
Some copies of the day's morning papers (if available).
Some copies of the list of social events and excursions organized by your school (if available).
Your own list of the members of each team and schedule for the simulation.
(If using video or a central 'studio' you need a proper microphone and so on.)

## Preparation

*This must be done several days before the simulation.*

*Talking points*

1 Talk about the questions as a class for a while.
2 Split the class into the teams they'll be in for the simulation and let them continue their discussion. Go from group to group joining in.
3 If you think it's necessary, look at the 'broadcasting expressions' on pages 10 and 34 of the Participant's Book.

*Before the simulation begins*

4 Get everyone to look at the notes and suggestions on pages 48 and 49 of their books. Allow enough time for the groups to meet again to decide exactly what they are going to do in advance and who's going to do what. Go from group to group, listening but not joining in, unless you feel they're getting nowhere.
5 Make sure everyone has been given a job to do for his or her group before you finish.

## The simulation

1 Show the teams to their rooms or areas and provide them with a cassette recorder and a blank cassette. Check that each recorder is in working order.
2 Announce the deadlines. These will all be the same if each team is recording as it goes along. Or they may be staggered if you're using video or recording in a central 'studio'. In the former case, the deadline is the time the recording must be finished by; in the latter, the time when each team must be ready to start recording.
3 Once the teams have started work, try not to interfere.

Eavesdrop if you like, make notes on the language errors you overhear, answer questions but only offer advice if you're specifically asked for it. Otherwise maintain a low profile.

4  If you're recording in a central 'studio', only allow one team to be present at a time. The teams who have finished can take a break while the later recordings are being done. Allow at least 5 minutes between each recording to absorb delays and technical hitches.

5  When all the programmes are recorded, ask the participants if they mind other students from another class being invited to the playback session. Respect their wishes. This invited audience is optional, anyway.

6  Take a 5 to 10 minute break. This can be longer if your timetable dictates it.

7  Reassemble to play back the recordings. Don't comment on broadcasting techniques or lack of professionalism. Just enjoy the shows together. Perhaps make notes of language points to mention afterwards.

8  Set the written work.

## Follow-up

Talk about the questions together. Make your own comments and suggest remedial work.

# Green Isle

## Description

The participants are divided into groups and each group has certain problems to solve connected with Green Isle. The exact nature of these problems is not revealed until the simulation has started. There may well be speculation among the participants as to what is going to happen, but resist all attempts to find out more. Keep a poker face if they make a lucky guess!

The *Green Isle* simulation has as its scenario the hijacking of a car ferry en route from Northbridge to Greenport by a group of 'Green Action Front' extremists. The participants represent hostages, crew and hijackers on the ferry, an emergency committee set up to deal with the situation and radio reporters who report on what happens. Each group occupies a separate area, preferably a separate room, and the ferry is isolated by being cut off from the other participants.

All communications between the rooms or areas must pass through the Controller's hands. In this simulation, the Controller's role is more active than in the others. The Controller has to evaluate all Messages and Proposed Moves and to decide on the Result of each Proposed Move. For example, if the Navy orders a submarine to torpedo the ferry, the Controller has to decide whether to allow the Proposed Move or to block it, depending on the state of the game at the time. The move can be blocked by announcing the Result as: 'Submarine engine fault – return to base.'

There is more advice on the Controller's role in the step-by-step instructions for the simulation. This is the most complex of the simulations and it should not be attempted before some of the earlier, more straightforward ones have been done.

The simulation provides the participants with an opportunity to discuss some important political issues. As the simulation is fiction, not reality, the participants can become deeply involved in the topic, without being forced into a real political confrontation with their fellow-students.

(Do not reveal *any* of this information to the participants!)

## Assigning roles and arranging groups

To help you to arrange the groups, the roles in this list are graded from '3-star' (essential) to 'no-star' (useful but dispensable):

| Group A<br>ON THE FERRY | Group B<br>IN THE EMERGENCY<br>COMMITTEE ROOM | Group C<br>IN THE RADIO<br>NORTHBRIDGE<br>NEWSROOM | Group D<br>IN THE RADIO<br>LYMPORT<br>NEWSROOM |
|---|---|---|---|
| *Hijackers*<br>★★★Harris<br>★★★Holmes<br>★★Hitchcock<br>★Harvey<br>Hopkins | *Police*<br>★★★Barlow<br>★Watt<br><br>*Royal Air Force*<br>★★★Armstrong<br>★Alexander | *Reporters*<br>★★★Norris<br>★★★Norman<br>★★★Newton<br>Nash | *Reporters*<br>★★Lucas<br>★★Lloyd<br>★★Lewis<br>Lawrence |
| *Crew*<br>★★★Carlton<br>★★Clarke | *Royal Navy*<br>★★★Russell<br>★Robertson | | |
| *Passengers*<br>★★Pritchard<br>★★Powell<br>Porter<br>Pickering<br>Perkins | *Home Office*<br>★★★Smith<br>★Jones<br><br>*Oil Refinery*<br>★★Sullivan<br>Gilbert | | |

The '3-star' roles are the minimum needed for a simulation of ten participants: there would only be one radio station and the hostages would be imaginary in this case.

With twenty participants the seven 'no-star' roles would be omitted and also three of the '1-star' roles, perhaps three of the seconds-in-command in the Emergency Committee Room.

In forming well-balanced groups, you need to consider the relative aggressiveness or reasonableness of your participants. This doesn't mean your five most aggressive students should be the Hijackers, just that each group needs a variety of different personalities in it. Remind them that within their roles they should behave as they would if they were in such a situation themselves and that there is no need to become great actors.

The Radio Reporters have quite a demanding part to play, since they are required to use their initiative more than the other participants. This means that they should *not* be your weakest students.

There should also be a 'strong personality' among the Passengers, since they too may have to work hard to succeed in making their mark.

*Green Isle*

## Organizing time and arranging space

*Preparation*    The talking points, useful language and practice activities take about 45 minutes – longer if the language is unfamiliar and the practice leads on to other matters.

*The simulation*    For the simulation itself, an uninterrupted period of 1½ – 4 hours is needed. The participants must *not* be allowed to take breaks in case they have a chance to communicate unofficially with the members of other groups. If absolutely necessary, there could be staggered, segregated breaks when only one group is free at a time and the others are still 'locked in'.

The simulation finishes at the appointed time, whether or not any satisfying dénouement has been achieved. Since the Controller in this simulation can manipulate events to some extent, it is possible to round things off with some sort of climax (see the step-by-step instructions).

In this specimen timetable the whole simulation is fitted into 3 hours (9.00 to 12.00) or 1½ hours (19.00 – 20.30):

| | | |
|---|---|---|
| 9.00 | Play news broadcasts. | 19.00 |
| 9.05 | Send participants to their rooms. Give out role information and rules. Supply other equipment as necessary. | 19.05 |
| 9.20 | Simulation begins: discussions held, messages sent, broadcasts prepared etc. | 19.15 |
| 12.00 | End of simulation. | 20.30 |

For the simulation, you must have at least *two* rooms available. The room representing the ferry is sealed and no-one is permitted to enter or leave without the Controller's permission. The Emergency Committee and the two Radio Stations can use separate areas of another room but if you can find them a room each, they will find their work easier to concentrate on. The ferry room should be divided into three areas: one for the hijackers, one for the crew and one for the passengers.

*Follow-up*    The follow-up discussion takes 30 to 45 minutes.

## What you need

Six photocopies of the rules of the simulation (page 129), one for each group. More copies might be useful.
Photocopies of the role information sheets (pages 130 to 137) with names and titles added for each participant. Let each participant keep his or her own first name, like this:

122

Green Isle

> You are ...... *Admiral Manuel Russell* ......
>
> You represent the Royal Navy forces stationed at Lymport.

Here is a list of the complete names and titles of each role and the number of photocopies needed of the pages containing the role information sheets:

Page 130 (2 to 5 photocopies): *Harris, Holmes, Hitchcock, Harvey* and *Hopkins*

Pages 131-2 (1 photocopy each): Add the passengers, first names only.

Page 133 (1 or 2 photocopies): *Captain Carlton*
*First Officer Clarke*
*Chief Superintendent Barlow*
*Chief Inspector Watt*

Page 134 (1 or 2 photocopies): *Air Marshal Armstrong*
*Air Vice Marshal Alexander*
*Admiral Russell*
*Vice Admiral Robertson*

Page 135 (1 or 2 photocopies): *Smith, Home Secretary*
*Jones, Home Secretary's Chief Adviser*

Page 136 (3 or 4 photocopies): *Sullivan, general manager*
*Gilbert, chief engineer*
*Norris, Norman, Newton* and *Nash*

Page 137 (up to 4 photocopies): *Lucas, Lloyd, Lewis* and *Lawrence*

A supply of blank postcards or slips of paper for the participants to write their Messages and Proposed Moves on.

A cassette recorder for each room and a blank cassette for each of the Radio Stations.

The *Eight Simulations* cassette for playing the first radio news broadcasts.

Your own schedule for the simulation and a list of the participants and their roles.

## Preparation

*Talking points*

1 These talking points may be a bit 'heavy' for a light-hearted group of participants but it's worth spending a few minutes exploring the theme to show that the simulation isn't just a game which is unrelated to reality.

*Useful language and practice activities*

2　Even a very advanced class will probably benefit from the practice in both of the sections.

3　In section 2 (*deciding and announcing the decision*), it might be worth suggesting some useful expressions:

| | |
|---|---|
| Discussing and deciding: | *Why don't we...* |
| | *Could we...* |
| | *Would it be possible to...* |
| | *What would happen if we...* |
| | *What if we...* |
| Announcing decisions: | *We've agreed to...* |
| | *We think it'd be best to...* |
| | *What we're going to do is to...* |
| | *We intend to...* |
| | *There's no alternative but to...* |

*Before the simulation begins*

4　Make sure everyone looks at the map on page 53 of the Participant's Book and reads all the newspaper articles on pages 54 to 57. It may be helpful to run through any tricky vocabulary beforehand.

## The simulation

1　Before assigning roles, play the two Radio news broadcasts on the cassette to the assembled participants. Get everyone to look at the map on page 53 of their books as they listen. Here is a transcript of the two broadcasts:

 **Radio Northbridge News at 9 o'clock.**

'News has just reached us of the hijacking of the car ferry "City of Northbridge" in Northbridge Water this morning. The ferry, on its way from Northbridge to Greenport, is believed to be under the control of the "Green Action Front", a militant wing of the Green Independence Movement. The terrorists are expected to make a number of demands and are threatening to blow up the ship.

The ship is at present off Nacton Spit, very near to the oil refinery and oil terminal at Nacton. It is feared that an explosion will not only kill the passengers and crew of the ferry, but also cause the oil refinery to explode.

An Emergency Committee has been set up and is due to meet in a few minutes. The terrorists are expected to publish their demands very shortly. We will keep you informed of developments every half-hour.'

## Radio Lymport News

'A dramatic development in the explosive situation on Green Isle: a car ferry from Northbridge to Greenport has been taken over by a group of extremists calling themselves the "Green Action Front". According to reports coming in, the terrorists are holding the passengers and crew hostage and demanding that the Government agree to their demands. An Emergency Committee has been set up to deal with the situation. The committee includes members of the Royal Navy, the Royal Air Force, the Police Force and the Home Office. They are expected to take a hard line and to propose a plan which will put a stop to Green Isle terrorists once and for all.

As soon as we have more information, we shall report it in special bulletins throughout the day.'

2  Without further ado, give everyone their prepared role information sheets and send them to their rooms or areas. Tell them that the simulation won't start until they've read the role information sheet and looked again at the information and the map in the Participant's Book.
3  Put each group together and give them a copy of the rules of the simulation (photocopied from page 129) to read. Go round each group making sure everyone understands the rules.
4  Give each group a supply of blank postcards or slips of paper for them to write their Messages and Proposed Moves on.
5  Give the radio teams a cassette recorder and blank cassette each.
6  When everyone is ready (steps 1 to 5 may take up to 20 minutes), start the simulation. Only the Controller or the Assistant Controller is allowed to board or leave the ferry without permission (see rules of the simulation).
7  During the first 20 – 30 minutes there is likely to be confusion, bewilderment or inaction. This is only to be expected when people are thrust into an unfamiliar situation. So, don't panic! Certainly, don't interfere at this stage.
8  After the first 20 – 30 minutes you may need to remind each group that it's time they sent a Message or proposed a Move. Remember that these Messages and Proposed Moves must go to the Controller first. Here is some advice on how to deal with these messages and moves:

*Messages* Make a note of the important messages in order to keep track of the action. Before you pass a message on to its addressee, the Radio Stations should be told the content of the message. (The idea behind this is that radio messages can normally be picked up by anyone with a suitable receiver unless they are in code, that is.)

*Proposed Moves* When you are notified of a proposed move, you must decide on the results of that move and report that result to *all* of the groups. The result you decide may alter the course of the game or even bring it to a premature end. For example:

| PROPOSED MOVE: | *Send helicopter to land on car ferry with commandos on board. Signed: Emergency Committee* |
|---|---|
| RESULT: | Terrorists blow up ship |

Well, that'd be the end of the game, so it's not a good result if there's still plenty of time to go. So, a better result at an early stage of the game would be:

| RESULT: Helicopter crashes into sea. Terrorists threaten to kill hostages if another attack is made on them. |
|---|

Another example (a proposed move after one hour's play):

| PROPOSED MOVE: | *Hostages to be killed one by one. First hostage will be thrown into sea at 11.00. Signed: Green Action Front.* |
|---|---|
| RESULT: | Hostage thrown overboard and drowned. |

This is an interesting result at this stage. The 'dead' hostage could become Assistant Controller. Alternatively:

| RESULT: | Hostage thrown overboard and manages to swim to the shore. |
|---|---|

In this case, the escapee can be interrogated by members of the Emergency Committee and/or interviewed by the Radio

Reporters. After that he or she could join the Emergency Committee as 'Special Adviser'.

In short, as you will by now have gathered, the Controller is omnipotent. The Controller's aim should not be to wield his or her power despotically, rather:

a)  to keep the game going *and*
b)  to preserve life (because a 'dead' participant will have to be given a new role, or asked to help the Controller, or be sent home early!).

To liven things up, or perhaps to speed things up, here are a few 'external events' which you can announce or get a Radio Station to report, if necessary:

| | |
|---|---|
| *A storm:* | The weather forecast says that a violent storm is imminent. The car ferry is likely to be blown against the Oil Refinery. |
| *Prime Minister's Statement:* | The Government is prepared to agree to the hijackers' demands on the matters of the Police and the Prisons *only*. |
| *Demonstrations:* | A large crowd of Islanders resident in Northbridge are demonstrating outside the Emergency Committee Room, demanding independence for Green Isle. |
| *A Public inquiry:* | Parliament has ordered a Public Inquiry into the death of Jonathan Freshwater. |

You can invent similar 'external events' of your own to suit the state of the game. Inform the participants of these events in writing, on postcards or on slips of paper.

9  The Radio Reporters will be busy trying to interview members of the Emergency Committee, sending Messages to the Ferry to try to gain admittance and preparing reports on the Messages and results of Proposed Moves which the Controller has told them about. Their recorded news programmes are broadcast in each room as soon as they are ready. This should be every half hour but this is a target rather than a rule. As soon as you are handed a news broadcast cassette by one of the Radio Stations, take it to the Ferry and let the participants there hear it before you take it to the Emergency Committee and the other Radio Station to hear.

10   10 – 15 minutes before the end of the simulation, you may
be searching frantically for a nice satisfying ending to the
game, like allowing the Ferry to be destroyed or liberated.
Such a result would be your decision. The participants can
only propose a move. For example:

```
PROPOSED MOVE: Squadron of bombers ordered
                to attack ferry
                   signed: Emergency Committee

RESULT:        Ferry destroyed - no survivors
```

This result is too clear-cut. A better result and ending for the
game might be:

```
RESULT: Bombers will take off from their base when
the fog lifts. All planes grounded until then.
```

In other words, no participant has 'failed' in what he or she
has been trying to do throughout the simulation. The result
is then less of a disappointment.
11   End of the simulation. Allow a good, long break before the
follow-up discussion if you want to do it next. It's better to
do it another day, if it's convenient.

However, just in case the simulation gets out of hand, you
can keep the option open of stopping the simulation early,
taking a break and then doing the follow-up discussion after
a break.
12   Ask everyone to do the written work.

## Follow-up

1   Make sure everyone gets a chance to explain what they did in
the simulation. Since the groups were separated, the participants may have no idea what was going on in the other
groups.
2   Discuss the answers to the questions. Make your own
comments on language points you noticed and suggest any
remedial work which may be useful.
3   Discuss to what extent the simulation reflected any real-life
events.
4   Set the written work if you haven't already.

## Rules of the simulation

1 Messages must be written down and passed to the Controller for transmission to their destination.

2 No member of the Emergency Committee has access to the ferry. No Radio Reporter can board the ferry without a written invitation from the hijackers.

3 All PROPOSED MOVES involving external events, travel or use of force must be written down and given to the Controller. The Controller will announce the RESULT of these moves.

4 All discussion stops when the Radio News is being broadcast.

You are ..................................................

*You are a militant member of the 'Green Action Front'. You and your comrades have taken control of the car ferry. You are holding the crew and passengers hostage. You and your comrades have fixed explosives to various parts of the ship – you will blow up the ship if your demands are not met, or if you are attacked. You have no weapons – only the explosives. If you blow up the ship you can escape by lifeboat to Green Isle, where supporters will hide you.*

Here is the policy of your group on Green Isle's situation:

| | |
|---|---|
| PRISONS: | The British Government maintains several prisons on Green Isle to which dangerous criminals are deported from Britain. These criminals often escape and Islanders are frightened and sometimes attacked. These prisons must be closed down and the prisoners housed somewhere on the Mainland. |
| POLICE: | The Island police force is well-known for its brutality. The police on the Island are all Mainlanders, not Islanders. The Island should have its own local police force – the Mainlanders would be sent home. |
| JONATHAN FRESHWATER: | The British Government assassinated this man, who was the founder of the 'Green Independence Movement'. He was killed because he was too popular. There must be an independent inquiry into his death so that the truth is made public. |
| INCOME TAX: | Taxes are too high. Islanders are paying for Mainland motorways, universities, defence forces and bureaucrats. This is not fair as Islanders get no benefit. Taxes must be reduced. |
| RETIRED PEOPLE: | There are too many elderly Mainlanders on Green Isle. Your policy is to encourage them to return to the Mainland and to prevent further immigration in the future. |
| INDEPENDENCE: | The only way to achieve your aims is for Green Isle to be self-governing. Total independence from the UK is what you want. |

*First*, prepare a Message outlining your demands to the Home Secretary and send it via the Controller.

*Second*, discuss with your comrades whether you are prepared to compromise on any of your demands. Which are the most important demands and which are you prepared to forget about if necessary?

---

You are ........................ **PRITCHARD**

*You are a passenger on the car ferry, now being held hostage by the 'Green Action Front' terrorists. You are a retired naval officer returning to your home on the island.*

*You believe that the hijackers are cowards and that you and your fellow-passengers can overpower them.*

Discuss the situation with your fellow-passengers. Decide on the best way to deal with the situation before you talk to the hijackers.

---

You are ........................ **POWELL**

*You are a passenger on the car ferry, now being held hostage by the 'Green Action Front' terrorists. You are a tourist on your way to spend a fortnight's holiday on Green Isle.*

*You believe that the only way to be released is to sympathize with the hijackers and be pleasant to them.*

Discuss the situation with your fellow-passengers. Decide on the best way to deal with the situation before you talk to the hijackers.

---

You are ........................ **PORTER**

*You are a passenger on the car ferry, now being held hostage by the 'Green Action Front' terrorists. You are a businessman on your way to the island to set up a new factory there. There is a lot of unemployment on Green Isle and your factory would offer 500 new jobs.*

*You believe the best approach is to discuss matters with the hijackers and try to persuade them to release you.*

Discuss the situation with your fellow-passengers. Decide on the best way to deal with the situation before you talk to the hijackers.

You are ....................................**PICKERING**....

*You are a passenger on the car ferry, now being held hostage by the 'Green Action Front' terrorists. You have been sent to the island to investigate prison security on behalf of the Home Office.*

*You believe the hijackers are reasonable people and that they can be persuaded to drop some of their demands.*

Discuss the situation with your fellow-passengers. Decide on the best way to deal with the situation before you talk to the hijackers.

You are ....................................**PERKINS**.

*You are a passenger on the car ferry, now being held hostage by the 'Green Action Front' terrorists. You are on your way to Green Isle to visit your grandmother in hospital.*

*You are afraid the hijackers will kill you and themselves.*

Discuss the situation with your fellow-passengers. Decide on the best way to deal with the situation before you talk to the hijackers.

You are ...........................................

You represent the crew of the car ferry.

*You are being held hostage by the terrorists. They have fixed explosive charges to the ship which will explode if the engines are started.*

*You are responsible for the safety of the passengers. There must be no violence. You believe that the British Government must agree to some of the terrorists' demands. The terrorists are fanatics who will not hesitate to blow everyone up.*

Discuss the situation with the other hostages before contacting the hijackers. Are the hijackers reasonable people or are they all mad? Should you oppose them or pretend to be on their side?

---

You are ...........................................

You represent the Police Force.

*You were unwilling to have the Navy and Air Force involved in this affair, but the Home Secretary insisted. You still think that the police can deal with the matter without any help from them. After all, you have police boats and police marksmen at your disposal.*

*This is the first act of terrorism from the so-called 'Green Action Front'. If the terrorists can be caught alive, brought to trial and imprisoned, this may also be the last act of terrorism. If they are killed, their supporters will continue terrorist activities in the name of their dead comrades.*

*You think the Home Secretary should agree to some of the terrorists' demands, otherwise people will die.*

Discuss the situation with your colleague before the meeting in the Emergency Committee room. Decide how the police are going to deal with the emergency.

You are ...............................................

You represent the Royal Air Force station at Northbridge.

*In your opinion, Admiral Russell and his colleague are typical Navy men: timid, never prepared to take risks, always ready to sit back and let things happen. These terrorists are a damn nuisance as far as you're concerned. You think they should be shot. Military operations should be kept secret from the public. You don't want the Press interfering.*

*You think the Home Secretary should not agree to any of the terrorists' demands.*

Discuss the situation with your colleague before the meeting in the Emergency Committee Room. Decide how you intend to deal with the emergency in the best RAF tradition.

---

You are ...............................................

You represent the Royal Navy forces stationed at Lymport.

*In your opinion, Air Marshal Armstrong and his colleague are typical Air Force types: reckless men who take too many risks.*

*You see the need for discretion and secrecy in communication with the terrorists, but it will be good for your future career if you handle matters successfully. It's important, therefore, for the public to be kept informed about developments, so that everyone knows you are acting wisely. You think the Press should be allowed to attend your meetings. If the other Committee members won't agree to this, you believe that the Press should be informed of all decisions the Committee makes.*

*You think the Home Secretary should agree to some of the terrorists' demands.*

Discuss the situation with your colleague before the meeting in the Emergency Committee Room. Decide how you plan to deal with the emergency in the best Royal Navy tradition.

You are ......................................................

*The Home Secretary represents the Government at the Emergency Committee and takes full responsibility for any actions the committee recommends.*

This is the Government's view of the Island's situation:

| | |
|---|---|
| PRISONS: | There are several important prisons on Green Isle. Dangerous criminals often escape from them. Security is getting worse. You have tried unsuccessfully to tighten it up. No other county in Mainland Britain would accept these prisons. |
| POLICE: | The Green Isle police force have been brutal. This is because most of them were recruited from the Mainland and are poorly trained. An all-Islander police force would be possible, but very expensive. The Prime Minister wants a tough, repressive police force on the Island. |
| JONATHAN FRESHWATER: | There can be no inquiry into the death of Freshwater. He was assassinated on Government orders. The official story is that he fell down a mineshaft while out walking – in fact he was pushed down. |
| INCOME TAX: | Green Isle is part of the United Kingdom. There can be no 'tax havens' as close as Green Isle is to the Mainland. |
| RETIRED PEOPLE: | There are thousands of elderly Mainlanders resident on Green Isle. Their interests must be protected. The last election proved that only a minority want independence. |
| INDEPENDENCE: | The Government's policy is to resist any attempts to split up the United Kingdom. A certain amount of self-government is allowed and Green Isle already has control of its own education, transport and public services. |

Discuss the situation with your colleague before meeting in the Emergency Committee Room. Decide how you intend to deal with the situation.

You are ..............................................

You work at the oil refinery.

*The car ferry is very near to your installations and the oil terminal where the tankers unload. If there is an explosion, the whole oil complex will go up too. This would be a major disaster. Many lives would be lost and millions of pounds of damage would be caused – not to mention the pollution.*

Discuss the situation with your colleague before the meeting in the Emergency Committee room. Decide how to protect your company's interests.

You are ..............................................

You are a radio reporter working for Radio Northbridge.

*Your listeners must be fully informed of developments as they happen. Your news broadcasts go out every half-hour. You can record reports and interviews on cassette for the news programme. This programme is heard by the Emergency Committee and the car ferry. (When your news cassette is ready, hand it to the Controller.)*

*Most of the listeners to Radio Northbridge sympathize with the 'Green Independence Movement'. The station is heard by Islanders on Green Isle and the large number of Islanders working in Northbridge. The station's policy is to present a balanced view, but you and the rest of the staff are sympathetic to the GIM.*

Discuss the situation with your colleagues. Decide who is to be responsible for each job before you try to make contact with the Emergency Committee (or with the hijackers).

You are ..............................................

You are a radio reporter working for Radio Lymport.

*Your listeners must be fully informed of developments as they happen. Your news broadcasts go out every half-hour. You can record reports and interviews on cassette for the news programme. This programme is heard by the Emergency Committee and the car ferry. (When your news cassette is ready, hand it to the Controller.)*

*Most of the listeners to Radio Lymport do not sympathize with the aims of the 'Green Independence Movement'. Their view is that they are all fanatics whose opinions are not shared by the majority of Green Isle's inhabitants. Many of your listeners are retired people from the Mainland living on Green Isle. The station's policy is to present a balanced view, but you and the rest of your staff are very much against the GIM.*

Discuss matters with your colleagues. Decide who is to be responsible for each job before you try to make contact with the Emergency Committee (or with the hijackers).